A Year in the
Country

A Year in the
Country

FRONT COVER
Cowboy on ranch in the Rocky Mountains, Telluride, Colorado
Pat & Chuck Blackley

PREVIOUS PAGE
Sunset over wetlands and meadow, Templeton, Massachusetts
Paul Rezendes

© 2018 RDA Enthusiast Brands, LLC.
1610 N. 2nd St., Suite 102, Milwaukee, WI 53212-3906

International Standard Book Number: 978-1-61765-749-8
International Standard Serial Number: 2576-3679
Component Number: 116800013H

TABLE OF CONTENTS

Spring

8   The Good Life

18   Scrapbook

32   Heart & Soul

38   Country Memories

39   A Taste of Spring

46   Handcrafted with Love

Summer

50   The Good Life

60   Scrapbook

78   Heart & Soul

88   Country Memories

89   A Taste of Summer

96   Handcrafted with Love

Autumn

100   The Good Life

110   Scrapbook

126   Heart & Soul

134   Country Memories

135   A Taste of Autumn

142   Handcrafted with Love

Winter

146   The Good Life

154   Scrapbook

168   Heart & Soul

176   Country Memories

177   A Taste of Winter

188   Handcrafted with Love

DAVID JENSEN

Welcome...

I f you long for the freedom of wide-open spaces, the magic of night skies filled with stars and the certainty of a person's word being their bond, then you have the right book in your hands.

A Year in the Country is an ode to the best of rural America. This keepsake volume follows the seasonal rhythm of country life with photos and stories from *Country, Farm & Ranch Living, Country Woman* and *Birds & Blooms* magazines.

You'll read about folks who still make a living off the land and don't mind a little dirt under their fingernails. You'll learn about communities where neighbors help each other and kids are free to stomp in mud puddles, cuddle with critters and roam until the sun goes down. These stories are authentic and heartfelt, told by the people who lived them.

Each section is filled with gorgeous photos that take you on a visual journey through America. Most of the nearly 300 images were shot by readers, whose pictures give you a candid glimpse into their lives and the beauty of the places they call home.

As a bonus, we've included seasonal recipes from country cooks and easy crafts that help make a house a home. No matter where you live, you can bring the best of the country to your table or turn your holiday celebration into an event.

If you ever need a reminder of all that remains good and true, just pick up this book, sit back, and escape to the country. — *The Editors*

The rising sun gently
awakens the wildflowers in
Idaho's Caribou Mountains.
Photo by Leland Howard

Spring

Take in the freshness of a season
full of new beginnings.

The Good Life

APPRECIATE THE SIMPLE PLEASURES

Flower Child

With the seed of caring for nature sown within me, I took root at my family farm at a young age. It was a process to be expected—my roots here go deep, back to my great-grandfather Anthony Sadlowski, who bought this 42-acre farm in 1942 with his wife, Julia.

Under my great-grandparents' care, the Sadlowski Farm raised livestock and grew vegetables, as well as tobacco as a cash crop. Two generations later, my father, Jeff, still grows tobacco and asparagus through the multigenerational efforts of the whole Sadlowski family. But along with the barns, corncrib and greenhouses that stick out among the tall, broad tobacco leaves and vertical asparagus spears, rows and rows of colorful ranunculus and lilac blooms clamor for attention at this time of year, while zinnias and sunflowers get their spring start nearby.

Sadlowski Farm—or part of it, anyway—has become Rooted Flower Farm, where we grow floral bouquets and sell them though a Community Supported Agriculture model. But even the roots of this venture stretch deep.

When I was a little girl, I couldn't be stopped from running barefoot over to Grammy's house or visiting my *babci* (great-grandmother) to see what was cooking. I'm rooted to this lifestyle and the sense of community that comes with it.

I'm rooted to the smell of the dirt and the possibility of nature. Some of my earliest memories are of sowing seeds in the greenhouse while my father prepared the garden. It wasn't long after I lost the training wheels on my bike that he started planting corn for my sister and me to pick and sell by the roadside. I tried to convince her that we could use the money to buy more seeds, but she settled with taking the cash instead.

In middle and high school, I carved my own path on the farm by growing a variety of fresh vegetables. After completing college, the love of growing and selling through my family farm stand expanded along with its offerings.

Rebecca's customers inspired her to grow flowers.

Rooted Flower Farm began as one row of flowers to supplement the vegetables at my stand. One row was followed by two, then three rows and so on over the years as I developed a love of flowers that continues to flourish.

The people visiting our farm stand got my gears turning about flowers. They wanted locally grown blooms, but few knew of a farmer who grew specialty flowers to sell directly to her customers. (According to industry advocates, nearly 80 percent of the U.S. flower market is imported, with little attention given to growing practices.)

Driven by my love for this land, I knew that I had found my niche and wanted to support the budding local-flower renaissance by becoming a source in my area for sustainably grown cut flowers. This led me to the CSA model, and Rooted Flower Farm was born. I went from growing acres of vegetables to specializing in just under a half-acre of cut flowers.

In our CSA, members pay at the onset of the season for a share of the flowers we will grow. I harvest flowers at their peak time and then carefully select and craft them into beautiful, colorful bouquets that members pick up

every week. Their investment helps to purchase seed and supplies, repair farm equipment and improve the farm's infrastructure. In return, the shareholders receive the freshest blooms possible, many of which are heirloom varieties that, because they don't ship well, are not found in stores. My CSA customers also gain an education about what is truly in season for our climate and region.

Rooted Flower Farm is a tribute to those who came before me and those who are with me as I continue to grow. It is my first love. As I harvest this season's beauties, I think about the seed that sprouted in me all those years ago, and I love to share the cuttings from those roots.

Rebecca Sadlowski
Hadley, Massachusetts

The Awakening Earth

There's no doubt that spring is my favorite season of the year. That's when I have an intense urge to be outdoors for fear of missing something new in the ever-changing landscape.

The grass turns a brilliant shade of green and so do the emerging leaves of trees and shrubs. Everything springs to life in an orderly fashion. I soak up the sun's warmth and the beauty of each new flower as I thank God for these marvelous creations.

Though spring has many false starts and always seems slow to come to Indiana, there's nothing more exciting than observing the first marble-shaped winter aconites emerge in late February. Their shiny yellow petals unfold in spite of the chilly air.

Snowdrops follow suit. Early morning frost often flattens these dainty white blossoms, but they rise bravely and open with the warmth of the sun.

After the long, drab winter, it always seems the colors of spring are prettier than the previous year's. It's so refreshing to see bold, vibrant hues awaken the landscape.

Generally, by the time my crocuses, hyacinths, daffodils, creeping phlox and tulips bloom, outside temperatures are more moderate. This year was an exception. Morning after morning, frost wilted my beautiful blooms. But those plants are amazingly tenacious, and spring's color parade marched on.

When I experience the faint fragrance of winter aconites, snowdrops and magnolias each spring, I believe they must be the loveliest scents. Later, when the yard is filled with lily of the valley, lilac, viburnum and mock orange, I am reminded that I could never pick a favorite, because each of them is a gift to my senses.

When the season is at its peak, I adore the lavish blooms of the redbud and crab apple trees, and I look forward to the seasons ahead, the stunning summer flowers and fall foliage.

Still, I cherish springtime most of all, because the awakening earth is a sign of new beginnings.

Kathe Bryant
Plainfield, Indiana

Daffodils are a cheery harbinger of spring.

Kaya, Peggy's granddaughter, offers Rosemary a cracker.

Leader of the Pack

My husband, Bill, and I moved to a little farm in the Ozark Mountains for our retirement years. It was his dream and I was just going along—grudgingly—for the ride.

But was I ever surprised! Now I absolutely love this farm life and, most of all, the animals. We raise Katahdin sheep, alpacas, pygmy goats, laying hens and Jersey dairy cows.

Rosemary the sheep is my favorite animal on the farm. She was the final lamb born in the spring, and the smallest. She has a birthmark that looks like a teardrop on her left eye. I named her after my mother.

The bigger lambs went more quickly to the feed trough and never left room for Rosemary. She didn't grow as fast as they did. Then she got sick and we spent some time nursing her back to health. Bill decided we would keep her for a pet and never sell her.

So we put Rosemary in the barnyard with our two livestock guardian dogs, Samson and Delilah, and our two older pygmy goats. After a few days of chasing her around, the dogs became fast friends with Rosemary.

The only problem was that after a while, our pet lamb began acting like a dog. When Samson and Delilah chased the goats around, Rosemary joined the fun.

I said, "Rosemary, sheep don't chase other animals." Next she began putting her two front legs up on me to beg for treats. "Rosemary, you're a sheep. Don't beg like the dogs do."

Then we bought two baby goats and put them in the barnyard with Rosemary, the dogs and older goats.

The babies began following Rosemary around and made her their new mother. Rosemary seemed to relish all of the special attention.

She even became part of the notorious "West Pasture Gang" for a while. Out in the west pasture, to the left of our house, we have put our silly and sassy assortment of female pygmy goats—Louise, Thelma, Peggy, Taylor Swift and Lola. They parade down the fence line in the morning to seek out new grass to eat, and parade back in the evenings to settle down for the night at the barnyard gate. I said to Bill, "Rosemary can't decide whether she's a dog or a goat."

When we got our new ewe lambs, Bill and I put Rosemary back in the pasture with them. We thought that she might fit in because they were younger than her. But for three days and three nights, she stood at the barnyard gate gazing at her beloved dogs and goats. I was afraid we had ruined poor Rosemary from ever being a sheep.

But like any good story, this one has a happy ending. After a few days, Rosemary decided she would be a sheep. In fact, she's the leader of the pack. The little lambs follow Rosemary wherever she goes.

She gets the choicest grasses and gets to be first at the feed trough and first in line for water, too. She seems happy and peaceful. Like Rosemary, I think we all need to find a place where we belong and where we feel loved and accepted.

Peggy Gray
Farmington, Arkansas

▶ I kept three dairy goats last spring, and I'm looking forward to raising my next herd of kids. The hours are long, but raising goats brings sweet rewards.

Grace Gardner
Grand Junction, Colorado

◀ My donkey Wilber was like a big dog. I was in love with him and will never forget him.

Staci Greene
Ramona, California

From Coop to Co-Op

If you have the privilege of owning chickens, you may be familiar with "chicken math." For those who aren't aware of the concept, let me explain. Once you become a proud chicken mama or papa, a phenomenon occurs where you feel an intense need to expand your brood. If you aren't careful, a few starter chickens can turn into eight or 12 or 20. I kept this in mind and restrained myself when the time came to make my first poultry purchase.

I had wanted chickens for a while, but one thing or another had always held me back. *Chickens are smelly,* I'd think. *Chickens like to scratch. They'll dig up the mulch in your flower beds. You don't have a coop. You can still buy eggs at the grocery store, can't you?*

Then my husband and I moved to a farm with an existing coop and a fenced-in yard. I could visualize my chicken idea turning into reality. I definitely wanted Rhode Island Reds, and I definitely wanted laying hens—no roosters. After a bit of searching, I welcomed five lovely ladies into my family: Henrietta (the head hen), Amber, Lucy, Scarlet and Ginger. They settled in and rewarded me with fresh eggs.

I vowed not to acquire any more chickens until the following spring, but I still had a dilemma. If I did get more chickens, what would I do with all of the extra eggs? A few of my friends also liked the thought of fresh-laid eggs, but either didn't have the right space or lived in a town where chickens weren't allowed. An idea began to form. Why not turn my chicken coop into a chicken co-op?

It is a simple model. Each person pays a membership fee to acquire a share. This covers the cost of a hen and monthly expenses for their food and care. Members name their chickens, get pictures of their chickens, visit their chickens and, of course, receive fresh eggs.

Although my father-in-law still likes to claim I'm running some type of chicken Ponzi scheme, I assure you that the co-op is quite honorable.

The co-op members and I researched breeds, and then we took a vote. We selected the Golden Laced Wyandotte, and soon enough, a group of fluffy sisters with shiny black and gold feathers arrived. Henny Penny, Audrey Henburn, Jennifer Heniston and Cleopatra quickly established themselves as members of our flock. Then, after patiently waiting and watching, came the prize. Little Henny Penny presented us with the co-op's first egg: extra small, brown, perfect.

Shellie McSloy
Cincinnatus, New York

Shellie's red coop (above) is home to all of the group's chickens.

► These cattle egrets moved from one neighbor's dairy cows to another neighbor's sheep. The sheep didn't seem to mind at all.

Richard Cronberg
Wildomar, California

▼ Llamas will sit during transport, unlike horses and cows, so ours were delivered in a Chevy Astro minivan. We have a blueberry farm, so we named them after the Blues Brothers—Jake and Elwood.

Jenna Hammerich
Oxford, Iowa

Dairy farming isn't just about producing milk and cheese. We're also major contributors to the beef industry at our farm.

Lisa Ruble
Waterford, Ohio
Photo by Michele Coleman

▲ Jake and Henry pick strawberries on the farm owned by their parents, Jordan and Steve Berryman.

Melissa Face
Prince George, Virginia
Photo by Amy W. Carroll

◄ A beekeeper opens the wax-capped honeycombs with a hot knife and lets the honey flow.

Melinda Myers
Mukwonago, Wisconsin

A Girl's Best Friend

I can't be the only girl in the whole world who believes that muck boots are the "little black dress" of rural footwear. These rubber boots are watertight, warm and shiny (when clean) in that just-sprayed-with-a-hose sort of way. And they will never let you down.

As a country girl, I relied on my boots for just about everything: wading in a crystalline river to catch crawdads, hurtling through white fields to avoid an onslaught of enemy snowballs and, believe it or not, some actual mucking around the yard of our home.

Country life is better in boots.

Though my farmstead soul has since been plopped down in the middle of a subdivision, I remain a country girl at heart and, perhaps unconventionally by city standards, a country girl in footwear. That's right: My muck boots are still with me, snuggled up like a hibernating bear in my suburban garage, waiting for the day when they touch soft, sweet prairie soil again.

I've dragged these muck boots through four houses, three states and plenty of misadventures. My parents bought them for me when I was just 10 years old, before farriers or chicken coops meant much of anything to us. The boots were on the shelf of our farm supply store, gleaming black under fluorescent lights and radiating ideals such as hard work and modesty. Drawn in by fantasy rather than function, everyone in my family got a pair.

They were big and awkward, swallowing my legs up to the knee with every step. Growing into them was a journey I undertook right alongside growing into my farming lifestyle. Looking back, I see that both were among the best things I've ever done.

Once I got used to the plunk-plunk-plunk rhythm of walking in muck boots, I abandoned all other footwear. I put more miles on those boots than I put on my first truck.

A move to the city demanded that I upgrade my footwear. While they were functional and left me unbeaten in every game of tag I'd ever played, my big black rubber boots were a liability in high school. However, I didn't get rid of them. I kept my boots in the garage, and to this day, I still find uses for them. A fall trip to the pumpkin patch. Shoveling snow. Playing with a huge, goofy St. Bernard in a muddy backyard. My boots have been there for me in the city just as much as they were in the country.

These days when I walk past the old muck boots, all scuffed up and more gray than black, I see a strange and bittersweet reflection of those sweet early years of my life. Somehow those boots are good at holding on to memories.

I still feel the thrill of running down a grassy hill at top speed, the peaceful pleasure of swinging booted feet over the side of a barn roof, the happiness of leading a loyal horse.

Like me, my sturdy boots are a fundamentally country thing dropped into a city lifestyle. Like me, they're making the best of it. They're never going to forget, and neither am I.

Ashlee Sierra
Boise, Idaho

RUBBER BOOTS: TRADERJ/SHUTTERSTOCK

Scrapbook

CAPTURE THE BEAUTY AROUND YOU

This brilliant double rainbow appeared over our property after a spring storm.

James Doughty
Hot Springs, Arkansas

Our granddaughter, Morgan, wore a pretty spring dress to visit her buddy Si in our friends' pasture. She has ridden the gentle giant in local horse shows.

Kim and Sam Warren
Blairsville, Georgia

"Is there anything better than growing up on a farm? I learned a lot about freedom and responsibility. Every day was an adventure."

Melissa Hartner
Monticello, Minnesota

▲ We bought this Jersey calf in the winter. It was too cold to haul him in the back of the truck, so he rode in the front cab where it was nice and warm!

Lorianne Ende
Rogers, Minnesota

My helpers wear their barn boots while doing chores every day. Simple moments like this one are why I love raising my boys in the country.

Tiffany Carter
Dansville, New York

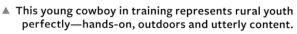

▲ This young cowboy in training represents rural youth perfectly—hands-on, outdoors and utterly content.

Todd Klassy
Havre, Montana

▶ An 11-week-old blue heeler named Waylon Blue Shugart is surrounded by spring flowers in bloom.

Sandra Shugart
Brentwood, Tennessee

A windmill stands like
a sentinel, watching
over the farm.
Annette Hillard
Danville, Illinois

Don't be afraid to leap.
You can't cross a chasm in two small jumps.

A gray day in March was a little brighter because of this sunny yellow warbler.

Roxanne Morgan
Hokah, Minnesota

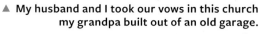

▲ My husband and I took our vows in this church my grandpa built out of an old garage.

Breanna Butler
Marshfield, Wisconsin

▶ Little Poquita was just 8 hours old in this photo. Her ears were already almost as big as those of her mama, Chili Burro.

Pat Graves
Dripping Springs, Arizona

While heading home on a rainy day, our daughter, Sienna, jumped in a mud puddle.
Raymond and Andrea Parmalee
Poulsbo, Washington

I noticed a bit of a glow in the sky one evening and went out to find the northern lights and the Milky Way lighting up the sky. After looking at my pictures, I saw a meteor in this photo. What an exciting night!

Katherine Plessner
Verona, North Dakota

▲ I like to imagine that someone out for a bike ride stopped to enjoy the beautiful flowers.

Annette Archuleta
Friendswood, Texas

◀ While out for a walk, my grandson Brady and I came across this field of dandelions. Brady decided to pick some for his mommy. What a thoughtful boy!

Nancy Saunders
Herkimer, New York

► One day, my fiancee, Brittany, and I took our dog to play in a field of bluebonnets. It's a tradition here in Texas; it just wouldn't be spring without seeing a bluebonnet patch. And Minnie had so much fun!

Daniel Andrade
Hitchcock, Texas

▲ I liked the sweet way this kid was looking at her mom. We named her Noel because she was born around Christmas.

Tanja Hupp
Mount Crawford, Virginia

▲ My daughter Anna likes to chase her feathery friends (like her chicken, Clementine) and give them big hugs.

Jessica Wagner
Versailles, Ohio

▶ When all the baby animals arrive in spring, it's such a joy to watch the children react to them. With a crown of flowers on her head, my niece gave these chicks a warm welcome.

Lorianne Ende
Rogers, Minnesota

▼ Spotsy is shown here with his mom, Joyce. The kitten, along with his brother, grew to be a great farm cat.

Daleen Cowgar
Norton, Ohio

▲ The sun peeks around granite boulders on the eastern shore of Lake Tahoe, Nevada.

Photo by Dennis Frates

◀ My great-niece Nora took her brother's Farmall tractor for a spin on her first birthday. She couldn't reach the pedals, but she sure did have fun.

Sue Krahn
Wykoff, Minnesota

Dusk adds drama to Burnt Jacket Point on Maine's Moosehead Lake.
Photo by Terry Wild

▲ My granddaughter Cassidy had her eyes on the ball during her first year of T-ball.

Nancy Mosburg
Franklin, Indiana

◀ Carrizo Plain National Monument, over 100 miles north of Los Angeles, has lots of agricultural history. This old tractor sits outside the entrance, and after years of driving by, we stopped when the conditions were ideal for this gorgeous shot.

Jody Langford
Templeton, California

▶ A bed of petunias nearly covers this old trunk next to my barn. These cheerful blooms really brighten up my day every time I see their lively display of color.

Gerald Yokely
Tobaccoville, North Carolina

▲ While visiting Gold Beach on the Rogue River, I had only a split second to snap a photo of this butterfly before it fluttered away.

RJ McBride
Independence, Oregon

Heart & Soul

FEEL THE LOVE OF COUNTRY

Ryan and his crew round up cattle on the Jones family's Montana ranch.

An antique tractor sits in a field outside of Broadus. Summer lightning flashes over the Yellowstone River (right).

Life in the Saddle

Sometimes you've got to deal with the elements, and that can get real tough here in eastern Montana. It's day in and day out—somebody's got to go feed the cattle and check on the water during winter. You've got to be committed to this way of life.

My family and I have worked this piece of land south of Miles City for over four decades. The Jones Family Ranch kind of borders the Tongue River. For the most part, this country is open and fairly rough. It's more like the Badlands of South Dakota than the Rocky Mountains of western Montana.

When the sun comes out, you see lots of colors in the heavy clay soil—whites, browns and purples. I'd never noticed the colors until my mother-in-law, who is a painter, came up from South Dakota and pointed them out to me. "Look at all the colors," she marveled. "What colors?" I asked, incredulous. Maybe I had been too busy moving cattle to notice.

The wildlife is diverse and the land is covered in sagebrush. Eastern Montana is ideal terrain for raising cattle. Most of the grass that grows out here is unsuitable for tillage, and there's not a lot of rainfall. Our livestock harvests the grass around here.

With its 10,000 residents, Miles City is the biggest town in the area. It's known as the Cow Capital of the West. The city, first called Miles Town, came to be after Gen. George Custer, many of his men and a number of Native Americans were killed in the Battle of Little Bighorn. The U.S. Army set up Fort Keogh at the confluence of the Tongue and Yellowstone rivers. The fort became a remount station, providing horses to the Army well into World War I. Today, the fort is a livestock and range research laboratory.

Miles City is steeped in the tradition of ranching, which goes way back to 1881 when the Northern Pacific Railroad reached what was then a military outpost. If you loved the television series *Lonesome Dove*, then you might remember that this is where the doctor amputated Gus McCrae's leg.

Another thing Miles City is famous for is hosting the Bucking Horse Sale. People who run rodeos come here to buy bucking horse stock, a tradition that goes back to 1914 when the Miles City Roundup began.

Like so many ranches out here, ours is a family-run operation. I work with my wife, Nicole, and my parents, Bill and Pansy Jones. We run about 200 mother cows, which makes us a midsize cattle operation. Our daughters, Laney and Riley, are still in school, but they are very much a part of the day-to-day operation of the ranch. In fact, they're members of the crew. Working with my family is what I love most about this way of life, because we don't just go our separate ways during the day.

Out here family is important, but so is community. When a member of the community reaches out to us in a time of need, we'll be there. It's an old-fashioned way of doing things, but it's how ranchers have survived in this rugged country.

An operation our size doesn't need full-time help—one cowboy can check on the cows while they graze. All the ranchers I know try to do it all themselves so they can keep labor costs down. But there are times when we need a few extra hands to finish big projects such as branding or shipping cattle. That's when I pick up the phone and call my friends and neighbors. Just about everyone makes it out here if they can. We all band together as a community and help each other get through these intense workloads.

One spring, my college roommate, brother-in-law, nephews and friends came out to the ranch to help with branding on a Saturday. I couldn't have hired a better crew. Among them were folks from around town who grew up on horses and learned to gather and sort at a young age. You don't get that kind of knowledge in a day. It takes years in the saddle, working with cattle.

Now, it's not always about the work. We try to find fun in what we do because ranching is our family time, too. I love watching my girls become an important part of the ranch. I don't know what Laney and Riley will be doing 20 years from now, but I hope they'll at least have the opportunity to carry on the legacy of the Jones Family Ranch.

The work is hard, but we do it because we enjoy it. I see the work I put in and the rewards of my labor. There's no better office than one with no walls, under a big blue sky.

Ryan Jones
Miles City, Montana

Ryan and Nicole's nephew Cole is one of the best hands on the crew.

Harvesting Humility

One spring day in 2015, my farmer husband of less than a year, Greg, asked this rookie farm girl to buy 12 sweet potato plants at the local garden center. He'd cultivated the garden and had visions of delicious sweet potato fries, casseroles and pies dancing in his head.

Eager to prove myself as a capable farmer's wife despite my suburban upbringing, I headed to the garden center and asked an employee to point me to the sweet potato plants.

"Sweet potato vines?" she asked helpfully.

"Sure," I responded, feeling a bit of doubt over the word vines.

I pushed my worries aside, wanting to appear as if I knew what I was doing. She pointed to a display and I confidently chose 12 hearty plants. I bought a large tray of sweet potato vines and drove back to the farm.

My father-in-law greeted me with a wry smile as he glanced at my armload of plants.

"I bought the wrong thing, didn't I?" I said.

Ever the diplomat, he shrugged his shoulders, and my sister-in-law took over the conversation.

"Oh, well!" she said. "If you've never seen sweet potato plants, you wouldn't know what to get."

Greg responded in a similar fashion, but sent me right back to the garden center.

On the short drive I pondered my new life; it felt hopeful and beautiful, yet also strange and awkward. In my previous two jobs—one focused on music and the other on public speaking—I had to be adept in performance, so confidence played a key role.

I suddenly realized confidence would not be vital to my success as a farmer. And in fact, overconfidence had gotten me into trouble. I needed humility, and the willingness to admit there was much I didn't know.

Back at the garden center, I exchanged my $20 worth of vines for $3 of sweet potato plants. To my surprise, the 12 new plants were tiny, about 6 inches long. I felt a little silly carrying this flimsy little cluster back to my car when earlier I'd emerged from it with arms full.

When I returned to the farm, I helped Greg plant, surprised that he'd made a dozen very large mounds of dirt—far larger than the plants I held in my hand. But, having learned my lesson, I kept my doubts to myself.

We harvested the crop several months later, Greg digging up the potatoes while I put them into empty seed sacks. The first sack filled quickly, and we soon filled a second—more than 200 pounds. I couldn't believe the 12 small plants provided an ample yield that included a huge, state fair-worthy sweet potato weighing 11.2 pounds.

Big results have come from living my new farm life with humility. I'm learning lessons and enjoying the rewards—like grilled sweet potato wedges.

Rachel Regier
Newton, Kansas

Much to her surprise, Rachel harvested an 11.2-pound sweet potato.

The ever-present flag on the barn (left) gave the Haugen family strength during a winter of waiting. Above, they welcomed Dad home from his deployment with signs, flags and love.

Beacon of Hope

The big red barn on our property has always been an important part of our family's life. Over the years, our three children spent many hours building forts in the haymow, playing hide-and-seek, and jumping into piles of hay. Angels were surely guarding our kids, cousins and friends from falling down the hay chutes and injuring themselves. What joy the kids had searching for new kittens hidden by Mama Cat or feeding newborn calves that sucked on their chubby little fingers. The 500-pound steers raised in that barn became pets and were proudly displayed at county fairs.

Our children now lead their own lives, but the cycle continues on the farm. Our five grandchildren are welcomed home to our big red barn to enjoy the same pleasures and adventures. Grampa Bryan proudly teaches them how to feed hay, care for the animals and, under his watchful eye, play in the haymow.

The summer of 2014 brought our children, grandchildren, friends and family to the farm to support our son, a pilot in the Minnesota Air National Guard. He was being deployed to the Middle East and we were sending him off with tears, hugs and prayers. Grampa Bryan

proudly attached a beautiful American flag to our big red barn. It was a symbol of our great nation, a reminder of the brave men and women who have fought for our freedoms, and a beacon to our son that would proudly be displayed until he returned home to his loved ones.

Summer heat gradually subsided and we welcomed the cooler temperatures and beautiful colors of autumn. The threat of winter brought on the race to harvest the crops, and long days followed with little rest. Every day we looked toward the flag on our barn and prayed for our son's safe return, and for his wife and three children who were waiting to see their daddy again.

An early snowfall turned our red barn white with ice and snow, making the red, white and blue of Old Glory stand out boldly.

Finally, we received word our son was coming home! We watched with joy and gratitude as his C-130 flew over the barn, dipping its wings to greet us and announce that he was back, safe and sound on American soil.

Laura Haugen
Dennison, Minnesota

Molly (below) was the second in a line of cows that helped teach Ashley many of the life lessons she hopes to share with her son, Derek (right).

Barnyard Classroom

Growing up on a dairy farm was not always as blissful and beautiful as people might picture. But it was emotional and educational, and it made me who I am today. I loved it.

Some of that education resulted from raising cows. During my childhood, there were special cows that taught me important life lessons. Memories of them bring a smile to my face and a tear to my eye.

It all started with Thunder, the first cow I recall bonding with. She was a big white Holstein who stood in the first stall in our barn. There was a gate next to her stall, and when I was about 4 years old, I used to climb up to brush her and talk to her while my parents did the milking. I spent hours brushing that cow. She was truly my friend, and I shared with her all my secrets and stories.

Then one day my parents told me it was time for Thunder to go to market. I didn't understand at the

time what that meant; I just knew Thunder was leaving, and I was devastated. I went on the trailer to give her one last hug. With tears rolling down my face, I watched as my pal rolled out of the driveway.

I learned from Thunder that cows are not pets. Though we may love them, their purpose is to provide food. When they can no longer give milk, they are meant to supply beef—a noble purpose.

Thunder taught me selflessness and nobility.

My first Jersey, Molly, was the next cow to teach me a valuable lesson. She was the only Jersey on our farm, and she had a huge personality. She had a hankering for Grandma's market tomatoes and could smell an open gate across the barnyard, a skill she would take advantage of any chance she got.

Despite her mischievous side, I showed Molly for six years at the county fair. We always did well, thanks to the special bond between us that the judges could see.

"During my childhood, there were special cows that taught me important life lessons."

When Molly was 4 years old, we had an exceptional year, and she was selected as the reserve grand champion Jersey of the 4-H show. With that huge shiny red trophy, I thought we were invincible. I was sure Molly was the best cow on the whole fairgrounds.

In the open show a couple of days later, we were handed the mustard-colored ribbon of fourth place. My first instinct was to blame the judge, who clearly didn't know what he was doing. After watching me pout for a while, my mother chatted with me about sportsmanship and modesty. Molly was a great cow, but she wasn't the "best" that day, and that was OK.

Molly taught me to be humble.

When I was 10, my father gave me a 6-year-old cow to show. Her name was Ginger, and she was a big beautiful black cow. She was set in her ways and really didn't want a little kid dragging her around a show ring. I worked hard that summer,

leading Ginger up and down our long driveway, sweating and panting with the effort. It was to no avail—the first year Ginger needed to be pushed around the whole ring. I was embarrassed, frustrated and ready to give up on her. But I kept working with her, and eventually that stubborn old cow gave in and decided she enjoyed the show ring. We went on for many years, even winning showmanship several times. Through Ginger, I learned that hard work and dedication pay off, and those achievements we work for the hardest yield the sweetest rewards.

Ginger taught me work ethic and dedication.

Since then, more cows have impacted my life, offering lessons through the bonds we forged. I hope someday my own son can tell a similar story from a life spent with animals on the family farm.

Ashley Abbott
Staunton, Virginia

Raymond's dad, Tom, (inset) took this reliable tin lunch box to work every day.

The Treasure Box

A cherished memento preserves Dad's legacy of hard work and family values.

Dad and his brothers grew up on a ranch in northern California, where they raised sheep and operated a sawmill in the nearby redwood forest. As a boy, I loved going to visit that sawmill.

One particular day stands out in my memory. Waking early, I joined Dad in the kitchen for breakfast as my stepmother, Ann, packed his beat-up tin lunch box with salami sandwiches wrapped in waxed paper, apples from our orchard and a mason jar of milk. Then we climbed into his ancient Model A coupe for the drive to the forest.

When we drew near the mill, I could smell smoke belching out of the teepee sawdust burner. Dad promised that if I behaved he would take me into the forest after lunch to watch him blow up a stump. Trucks,

bulldozers and dynamite all in one day! It was more than any 11-year-old could hope for.

I whittled a block of wood and watched my father work. Although he was only 5 feet tall, Dad easily moved the wood slabs. His arms looked like Popeye's, and I wanted mine to look the same way.

The sun rose to its peak and my stomach growled. Dad pulled the sandwiches out of his lunch box. I devoured mine in a few bites.

After lunch, I blurted out, "Ann says you need a new lunch box."

He explained that he had a new one, but he didn't use it because this box had belonged to his father.

My mind filled with visions of the things I could store inside it. So I mustered up a little courage and asked if I could have it. Dad said

maybe after he retired. I grew up, grew old, and in time I forgot about the lunch box.

A few years ago Dad passed away. He was 95 and had lived a good life. It didn't ease the pain.

The next summer, I received a package just before Father's Day. Inside was Dad's box with a note that said, "Son, I haven't forgotten that you wanted this lunch box. Keep it in the family, as it has been with us a long, long time—Dad."

I cried a lot that day, thinking about a time gone by when a young boy sat in the forest watching his family work. I've since passed the heirloom on to my own son. Dad's lunch box and its legacy of hard work will never leave us.

Raymond L. Prather
Rochester, Minnesota

A Taste of Spring

SAVOR THE FLAVORS OF THE SEASON

Berry Pinwheel Cake

PREP: 30 MIN. + CHILLING · **BAKE:** 10 MIN. + COOLING · **MAKES:** 8 SERVINGS

INGREDIENTS

- 4 large egg yolks
- 2 large eggs
- ½ cup sugar
- 2 tablespoons water
- 2 teaspoons canola oil
- 1 teaspoon vanilla extract
- 1 cup cake flour
- 1 teaspoon baking powder
- ½ teaspoon salt
  Confectioners' sugar

FILLING

- 1 cup heavy whipping cream
- 1 tablespoon sugar
- 3 tablespoons lemon curd
- 2 cups coarsely chopped
  fresh strawberries

DIRECTIONS

1. Preheat oven to 375°. Line the bottom of a greased 15x10x1-in. pan with parchment paper; grease paper.

2. Beat egg yolks and eggs on high speed for 3 minutes. Gradually add sugar, beating until thick and lemon-colored. Beat in water, oil and vanilla. In another bowl, whisk together flour, baking powder and salt; fold into egg mixture. Spread evenly into prepared pan.

3. Bake until top springs back when lightly touched, 10-12 minutes. Cool for 5 minutes. Invert onto a tea towel dusted with confectioners' sugar. Gently peel off paper. Roll up cake in the towel jelly-roll style, starting with a short side. Cool completely on a wire rack.

4. For filling, beat cream until it begins to thicken. Add sugar; beat until stiff peaks form. Fold in lemon curd. Gently fold in strawberries.

5. Unroll cake; spread filling to within ½ in. of edges. Roll up again, without towel; trim ends. Place on a platter, seam side down. Refrigerate, covered, 1 hour. Dust with confectioners' sugar before serving.

Horseradish-Glazed Ham

PREP: 15 MIN. • **BAKE:** 1 HOUR 40 MIN.
MAKES: 12 SERVINGS

INGREDIENTS

- 1 fully cooked bone-in ham (5 to 6 pounds)
  Whole cloves
- 1 cup packed brown sugar
- ⅓ cup prepared horseradish
- ¼ cup lemon juice

DIRECTIONS

1. Using a sharp knife, score surface of ham with ¼-in.-deep cuts in a diamond pattern; insert a clove in each diamond. Bake according to package directions.
2. Meanwhile, mix remaining ingredients. Brush over ham during the last 30 minutes of cooking.

Loaded Red Potato Casserole

PREP: 25 MIN. • **BAKE:** 20 MIN.
MAKES: 8 SERVINGS

INGREDIENTS

16 small red potatoes (about 1¾ pounds)
½ cup 2% milk
¼ cup butter, cubed
½ teaspoon pepper
⅛ teaspoon salt
1½ cups shredded cheddar cheese, divided
½ cup crumbled cooked bacon
1 cup (8 ounces) sour cream
2 tablespoons minced fresh chives

DIRECTIONS

1. Preheat oven to 350°. Place potatoes in a 6-qt. stockpot; add water to cover. Bring to a boil. Reduce heat; cook, uncovered, until tender, 15-20 minutes. Drain; return to pot.
2. Mash potatoes, gradually adding milk, butter, pepper and salt. Spread into a greased 13x9-in. baking dish; sprinkle with 1 cup cheese and bacon. Dollop with sour cream; sprinkle with chives and remaining cheese.
3. Bake, uncovered, until heated through and cheese is melted, 20-25 minutes.

Pea Soup with Quinoa

PREP: 10 MIN. • **COOK:** 25 MIN.
MAKES: 6 SERVINGS

INGREDIENTS

1 cup water
½ cup quinoa, rinsed
2 teaspoons canola oil
1 medium onion, chopped
2½ cups frozen peas (about 10 ounces)
2 cans (14½ ounces each) reduced-sodium chicken broth or vegetable broth
½ teaspoon salt
¼ teaspoon pepper
Optional toppings: plain yogurt, croutons, shaved Parmesan cheese and cracked pepper

DIRECTIONS

1. In a small saucepan, bring water to a boil. Add quinoa. Reduce heat; simmer, covered, until water is absorbed, 12-15 minutes.
2. Meanwhile, in a large saucepan, heat oil over medium-high heat; saute onion until tender. Stir in peas and broth; bring to a boil. Reduce heat; simmer, uncovered, until peas are tender, about 5 minutes.
3. Puree soup using an immersion blender. Or, cool slightly and puree soup in a blender; return to pan. Stir in quinoa, salt and pepper; heat through. Serve with toppings as desired.

Lemon Cranberry Quinoa Salad

START TO FINISH: 30 MIN. • **MAKES:** 8 SERVINGS

INGREDIENTS

- ¼ cup olive oil
- 2 teaspoons grated lemon peel
- 2 tablespoons lemon juice
- 2 teaspoons minced fresh gingerroot
- ¾ teaspoon salt

SALAD

- 2 cups reduced-sodium chicken broth
- 1 cup quinoa, rinsed
- 1 cup chopped peeled jicama or tart apple
- 1 cup chopped seeded cucumber
- ¾ cup dried cranberries
- ½ cup minced fresh parsley
- 1 green onion, thinly sliced
- 1 cup cubed avocado

DIRECTIONS

1. For dressing, in a small bowl, whisk the first five ingredients until blended.
2. In a small saucepan, bring broth to a boil. Add quinoa. Reduce heat; simmer, covered, 12-15 minutes or until liquid is absorbed. Remove from heat; fluff with a fork. Transfer to a large bowl.
3. Add jicama, cucumber, cranberries, parsley and green onion to quinoa. Drizzle with dressing and toss to coat. Serve warm or refrigerate and serve cold. Gently stir in avocado before serving.

Tuscan-Style Roasted Asparagus

PREP: 20 MIN. • **BAKE:** 15 MIN.
MAKES: 8 SERVINGS

INGREDIENTS

- 1½ pounds fresh asparagus, trimmed
- 1½ cups grape tomatoes, halved
- 3 tablespoons pine nuts
- 3 tablespoons olive oil, divided
- 2 garlic cloves, minced
- 1 teaspoon kosher salt
- ½ teaspoon pepper
- 1 tablespoon lemon juice
- ⅓ cup grated Parmesan cheese
- 1 teaspoon grated lemon peel

DIRECTIONS

1. Preheat oven to 400°. Place the asparagus, tomatoes and pine nuts on a foil-lined 15x10x1-in. baking pan. Mix 2 tablespoons oil, garlic, salt and pepper; add to asparagus and toss to coat.
2. Bake 15-20 minutes or just until asparagus is tender. Drizzle with remaining oil and the lemon juice; sprinkle with cheese and lemon peel. Toss to combine.

Hot Crab Pinwheels

PREP: 15 MIN. + CHILLING • **BAKE:** 10 MIN.
MAKES: 3 DOZEN

INGREDIENTS

- 1 package (8 ounces) reduced-fat cream cheese
- 1 can (6 ounces) crabmeat, drained, flaked and cartilage removed
- ¾ cup diced sweet red pepper
- ½ cup shredded reduced-fat cheddar cheese
- 2 green onions, thinly sliced
- 3 tablespoons minced fresh parsley
- ¼ to ½ teaspoon cayenne pepper
- 6 flour tortillas (6 inches)

DIRECTIONS

1. Beat cream cheese until smooth; stir in crab, red pepper, cheese, green onions, parsley and cayenne. Spread ⅓ cup filling over each tortilla; roll up tightly. Wrap in plastic, twisting ends to seal; refrigerate for at least 2 hours.

2. To serve, preheat oven to 350°. Unwrap rolls; trim ends and cut each into six slices. Place on baking sheets coated with cooking spray. Bake until bubbly, about 10 minutes. Serve warm.

Raspberry Sour Cream Coffee Cake

PREP: 20 MIN. • **BAKE:** 30 MIN. + COOLING
MAKES: 8 SERVINGS

INGREDIENTS

- 1 cup fresh raspberries
- 3 tablespoons brown sugar
- 1 cup all-purpose flour
- ⅓ cup sugar
- ½ teaspoon baking powder
- ¼ teaspoon baking soda
- ⅛ teaspoon salt
- 1 large egg
- ⅔ cup sour cream
- 3 tablespoons butter, melted
- 1 teaspoon vanilla extract
- ¼ cup sliced almonds

ICING
- ¼ cup confectioners' sugar
- 1½ teaspoons 2% milk
- ¼ teaspoon vanilla extract
  Additional raspberries, optional

DIRECTIONS

1. Preheat oven to 350°. In a small bowl, toss raspberries with brown sugar.

2. In a large bowl, whisk flour, sugar, baking powder, baking soda and salt. In another bowl, whisk egg, sour cream, melted butter and vanilla until blended. Add to flour mixture; stir just until moistened (batter will be thick).

3. Transfer half of the batter to a greased and floured 8-in. round baking pan. Top with raspberry mixture. Spoon remaining batter over raspberries; sprinkle with almonds.

4. Bake 30-35 minutes or until a toothpick inserted in the center comes out clean. Cool in pan for 10 minutes before removing to a wire rack to cool.

5. In a small bowl, mix confectioners' sugar, milk and vanilla until smooth; drizzle over top. Serve warm. If desired, serve with additional raspberries.

Roasted Radishes

PREP: 10 MIN. • **BAKE:** 30 MIN.
MAKES: 6 SERVINGS

INGREDIENTS

- 2¼ pounds radishes, trimmed and quartered (about 6 cups)
- 3 tablespoons olive oil
- 1 tablespoon minced fresh oregano or 1 teaspoon dried oregano
- ¼ teaspoon salt
- ⅛ teaspoon pepper

DIRECTIONS

1. Preheat oven to 425°. Toss radishes with remaining ingredients. Transfer to a greased 15x10x1-in. pan.

2. Roast until crisp-tender, about 30 minutes, stirring once.

Herb-Buttered Baby Carrots

PREP: 10 MIN. • **BAKE:** 50 MIN.
MAKES: 4 SERVINGS

INGREDIENTS

- 1 pound fresh baby carrots, trimmed
- ¼ cup butter, cubed
- 1 garlic clove, minced
- 1½ teaspoons minced fresh parsley or ½ teaspoon dried parsley flakes
- ¼ teaspoon dried basil
- ⅛ teaspoon dried marjoram
- ⅛ teaspoon dried oregano
- ⅛ teaspoon dried rosemary, crushed
- ⅛ teaspoon dried thyme

DIRECTIONS

1. Preheat oven to 375°. Place carrots in a greased 1½-qt. baking dish. In a microwave, melt butter; stir in garlic and herbs. Toss with carrots.
2. Bake, covered, until carrots are tender, 50-60 minutes, stirring once.

Green Salad with Dill Dressing

PREP: 20 MIN. + CHILLING
MAKES: 8 SERVINGS

INGREDIENTS

- 2 tablespoons sour cream
- 2 tablespoons red wine vinegar
- 2 teaspoons dill weed
- 1 teaspoon Dijon mustard
- ¼ cup canola oil
- 3 tablespoons olive oil
- ¼ teaspoon salt, optional

SALAD

- 4 cups torn romaine
- 2 cups torn Boston or Bibb lettuce
- 1 large green pepper, cut into strips
- 1 small cucumber, sliced
- 1 large tomato, chopped
- 1 carrot, shredded
- 4 green onions, sliced
- 3 radishes, sliced

DIRECTIONS

1. Whisk together first four ingredients; gradually whisk in oils and, if desired, salt until blended. Refrigerate at least 30 minutes.
2. In a large bowl, toss together salad ingredients; refrigerate, covered, until serving. Serve with dressing, stirring to recombine if needed.

Handcrafted with Love

CREATE A FEELING OF HOME

Special Delivery

Transform a vintage hankie into the perfect place to tuck a favorite family recipe with this craft from bumblebeelinens.com by Jennifer Chou.

WHAT YOU'LL NEED
- **Vintage embroidered handkerchief**
- **Coordinating thread**
- **Recipe cards**

DIRECTIONS

1. Lay the handkerchief flat with the back side of the embroidery facing up and pointed toward the top.

2. Fold the left corner of the handkerchief two-thirds of the way toward the right corner. Repeat with the right corner, folding toward the left. Fold the bottom of the handkerchief one-third of the way up; fold it upward again to create a pocket.

3. With a needle and thread, sew a running stitch along the two sides of the bottom fold, creating an envelope.

4. Fold the top corner of the handkerchief down to form the envelope flap. Tuck recipe cards into the envelope.

Top a Table

End-to-end hankies make a distinctive and dainty table runner.

WHAT YOU'LL NEED
- **Vintage handkerchiefs**
- **Coordinating lace trim**
- **Coordinating ribbon trim**
- **Coordinating thread**
- **Sewing machine, optional**

DIRECTIONS

1. Lay handkerchiefs side by side to reach desired length. Pin into place.

2. If using a sewing machine, sew one handkerchief onto the next. If using a needle and thread, use a running stitch to sew handkerchiefs together by hand.

3. Cut two pieces of lace the length of the runner's ends. Pin one piece of lace to the back side of each end. Sew lace trim behind the handkerchief ends.

4. Cut two pieces of ribbon trim the length of the runner's ends. Pin one piece of ribbon trim to the front side of each end. Stitch ribbon in place.

Spring Greening

Celebrate the season's renewal with this moss cross.

WHAT YOU'LL NEED
- **Wooden cross on stand**
- **Moss**
- **Wood stain**
- **Rag or foam brush**
- **Hot glue gun**

DIRECTIONS

1. Using a rag or a foam brush, coat the wooden cross with the wood stain.

2. Wipe off excess stain. Let dry.

3. Glue moss to the cross using a glue gun.

Summer

Bask in sunny days, warm breezes and the blessed bounty of the carefree season.

Light falls on fields and a barn
in Pleasant Ridge, Wisconsin.
Photo by Terry Donnelly

Dyersville, Iowa, is baseball heaven for the Clarkes.

For the Love of the Game

The doldrums of the off-season were broken suddenly on November 24, 2015, when the Murphysboro Clarkes received an invitation from Matt "Scoops" Lurk of the St. Louis Unions to join six vintage baseball teams at the Field of Dreams in Dyersville, Iowa. This news quickly spread among the team.

Within a few days, the Clarkes announced, "We're in!" and marked August 5-7, 2016, on the calendar.

The Clarkes have played vintage "base ball" (the old spelling) since our inaugural match on May 21, 2005. Vintage baseball honors and respects our country's favorite pastime, conducting matches according to the highest standards of sportsmanship, gentlemanly behavior, courtesy and respect for other people.

The ball is slightly bigger and heavier than a modern baseball. Players dress in old-time uniforms and do not wear gloves. And every player (*ballist*, we say) has a nickname that is either self-proclaimed or designated by a teammate, such as Dawg, Black Bart, Legs, Icy Hot, Junior, One Leg, Chief, Train, Bags, Wrongway, Old Man, Spike, Fast Action and Splat.

The rules are slightly different, too. Fair or foul is determined by where the ball first lands. A batter is out if the baseball is caught on one bounce. Base runners can't overrun first base but must stop on the bag. And swearing, wagering, spitting and scratching are not allowed. Violators are subject to a 25-cent fine, equivalent to a day's wages in the 1860s.

Spring of 2016 brought another baseball season, and with it, another trip back in time to honor history and community. Our schedule included matches with the Brown Stockings, the Perfectos, the Unions and the Lafayette Square Cyclone from Missouri; the Belleville Stags, Vandalia Old Capitals, Breese Shoal Creek Farmers, Vermillion Voles, Springfield Long Nine and Chicago Salmon from Illinois; and the Hog and Hominy Picked Nine from Tennessee.

The season progressed with trips to Jefferson Barracks Park and Emmenegger Nature Park, both in St. Louis, and matches at our hometown venue, Longfellow Park.

When the much-anticipated first weekend in August finally arrived, a caravan of Clarkes and our families departed southern Illinois with grand dreams of what would greet us in Iowa.

The 6½-hour trip seemed to take no time at all, as we were on our way to hallowed baseball ground. As our vehicle approached Dyersville, my heart raced with anticipation. Dark green corn as far as the eye could see bordered the last three miles of our journey. When we arrived, we were overcome with the aura of baseball history and all that is good about the sport.

Shoeless Joe, the book by W. P. Kinsella, and the movie *Field of Dreams* came to life on this grand weekend. For three days, all was right in our world as the Clarkes, Unions, Perfectos, Cyclone, Brown Stockings, Stags and Voles played out a tournament connecting the past and present. Our camaraderie demonstrated the genuine spirit of vintage baseball.

The weekend we took the field at this special place was another illustration for the Clarkes that baseball is hands-down the best game in town. The Field of Dreams in Dyersville exceeded our high expectations and unequivocally displayed why it's rightfully known as baseball heaven.

There, a bright blue sky, neatly manicured grass, endless rows of magnificent corn and beautiful weather combined to create the perfect setting.

Evening games were accentuated by a magical fog that settled across the outfield, calling attention to the sense of inspiration that hung in the Iowa air.

And in it, I reflected on the resplendent days of my youth, spending quality time with my dad, learning to play ball.

Jeffrey Wright
Murphysboro, Illinois

Fog made the night games seem particularly magical.

"When we arrived, we were overcome with the aura of baseball history and all that is good about the sport."

Players emerge from the towering corn stalks at the Field of Dreams.

Though Red Twig Farms peonies are harvested in May, cold storage allows the family to sell them into early July.

Lindsey and Josh lead a weeklong harvest every spring, during which the family hand-picks over 15,000 peonies.

A Handpicked Homestead

It's hard to believe that what is now 9 acres of gorgeous peonies, dogwoods and willows sat dormant for two decades. In 2010, my husband, Josh, and his family decided to buy the long-neglected property just across the street from their landscaping company. They planned to harvest the dogwoods and willows for landscaping use, but realized they needed a summer crop to increase sales. So they chose to grow peonies. At the time, they could not have imagined how fruitful that decision would turn out to be.

Peonies take a few years to mature before they can be harvested, so from 2010 to '13, the family worked the land and established the plants. Red Twig Farms was officially opened for business in 2013, the same year that Josh and I got married.

Every Saturday morning after we opened, I would head to the local farmers market to sell farm-fresh peonies with Josh and my father-in-law, Karl. It took only a few trips for our flowers to become the market's hot item, and we responded to the demand by opening a farm store in 2016.

Customers now stop by the farm to pick out bouquets and tour the flower fields. We grow peonies in six colors: white, coral, light pink, medium pink, dark pink and magenta. The coral variety is always the first to sell out. The store has been such a wonderful addition to the farm that it has become our main selling area, supplanting the weekly farmers market stall. Customers really seem to love getting their peonies from the source and seeing how the flowers are grown and harvested.

We harvest the peonies by hand in mid- to late May, checking every stem for quality. This means that we handle more than 15,000 peony stems by hand in a picking period of seven to 10 days. The peonies tell us exactly when they need to be harvested—the closed flower feels like a soft marshmallow—and then it's go time. The fields come to life with thousands of delicate pink, deep magenta, blush and coral buds on the verge of bursting open.

We harvest from early morning to late evening for several days. Once we're done harvesting, we place the cut peonies in cold storage to stop the blooming process.

Thanks to this process, we can sell flowers into early July even though the harvest may be completed in early June. We take flowers to local markets and florists, and each year we add varieties that were successful in our test plots.

While our peonies are our pride and joy, we also grow more than 3 acres of dogwoods and willows. These ornamental branches are harvested from late fall through the winter. We offer red and yellow dogwood and several different varieties of willow, including Golden Curls and Flame. The branches are great for floral arrangements, outdoor containers and woven structures such as baskets. Our pussy willow branches are flush in the fields through February and March. We grow a traditional variety with dark brown stems, as well as a special variety with buds that are tinted pink.

Josh and I built our home on the Red Twig Farms property in 2014. We both liked the look and symbolic meaning of a traditional farmhouse. When we walk around our home we smile, because even the smallest detail contains a personal story.

An amazing stonemason with a half-century of experience laid our fireplace stone. Our copper farmhouse kitchen sink continues to discolor from all the use at family get-togethers and holidays. Josh's late grandfather's spearmint is planted in our yard. His antique tools line our dining room hutch. I planted wildflowers over our septic field, and I love cutting fresh flowers whenever I want. These unique details help make our farmhouse special.

Red Twig is a small farm, and we haven't been in the flower business for very long, but we are full of heart. We strive to bring back meaningful traditions and create new memories. I can remember admiring the peonies that surrounded my great-grandmother's house when I was a child. Who could have known that I would grow up to be a peony farmer? Now that we sell peony plants in our farm store, we can help customers plant their own pretty memories.

Lindsey McCullough
New Albany, Ohio

▲ We were camping at Lincoln State Park near Santa Claus, Indiana, and on my morning walk around the lake, I admired this canoe nestled among the lily pads.

Maria Schulz
Floyds Knobs, Indiana

► After climbing out of Logan Pass in Glacier National Park, my granddaughter, Perse, and her best friend, Madison, were so thrilled to see this mountain goat and her baby.

Roger Dougherty
Kingsport, Tennessee

Monarch Madness

Although I'd heard about the declining numbers of monarch butterflies, I didn't know the whole story. And as a person who values the beauty and satisfaction of growing my own vegetables and flowers, I wanted to learn more about this issue.

During the winter of 2015, our local science museum featured *Flight of the Butterflies*, a film that documents the annual monarch migration from as far north as Canada to a specific mountain region in Mexico and back again.

After the movie, we visited the butterfly house to feed butterflies. There, we learned monarchs have been steadily declining, in part because of decreased availability of milkweed, their most essential food source.

That spring I learned as much as I could about raising monarchs. While opinions differ about how pesticides have contributed to the pollinators' decline, I know firsthand that caterpillars that feed on treated plants don't survive.

I didn't want any plants that had been treated with pesticides in the new pollinator garden I planned. So I purchased a variety of healthy plants from a local native grower to attract monarchs, bees and other endangered pollinators.

When the first shoots of common milkweed emerged, I was ecstatic. As the few milkweed plants grew, I protected them as though they were prized orchids. Then one day we saw a butterfly flitting from one plant to another. After she left, I found my first monarch eggs, and thus began my wonderful summer of monarch madness.

In 2015, I raised and released 64 monarchs—not too bad for my first year. Some eggs didn't hatch and some hatchlings died. Saddest of all were the caterpillars that struggled to emerge from the chrysalis and died in the attempt.

Monarchs thrive in Jeanne's garden.

I'm not embarrassed to tell you I cried over some of them. But I take heart knowing that in the wild, only a tiny fraction of the eggs I found would have become butterflies. And of those 64 little orange and black creatures that started life in my kitchen, maybe a few even made it all the way south to Mexico.

At the end of summer, I scattered the seeds from my wild milkweed farther into our field, hoping they would grow into a large wild patch. With any luck, my native garden will flourish in the coming years as a glorious haven for monarch butterflies and other pollinators, as well.

I really have a wonderful and satisfying hobby!

Jeanne Lundeen
Hugo, Minnesota

► Charley loves playing in the summer-tall corn.

Alisa Etzel
Park City, Montana

►► Small wonders delight the senses.

Laura Adrian
Hermosa, South Dakota

I love the way my brother, James Stokley, is smiling at his girls Saige (left) and Nichole from his spreader truck as they run to him. The love of family is so beautiful.

Stephanie Beard
Waynesboro, Mississippi

Picking and Playing

Sam smiles with delight at the fresh raspberries he picked to share with Mom.

The sound of children's laughter and the high-pitched squeal of an old swing set filled the sticky summer air as I rested on the only shaded bench at our small community playground. My feet were tired and my body ached from standing at work.

All I wanted to do was go home and crawl into bed, yet we remained at the humid playground. I knew my son, Sam, needed some playtime—and the more energy he burned now, the sooner he would fall asleep later.

Just as the heat was becoming unbearable, a sea breeze blew across the plastic towers and wood chips. It cooled my sweating skin and seemed to rejuvenate me in an instant.

"Hey, sweet boy," I said. "Let's pick some raspberries from the bush." Sam came running over, excited for a treat.

We live in a quiet neighborhood. A few summers back, one of the playground neighbors planted a small raspberry bush on the edge of their property. Each year it has doubled in size, and now a patch extends into the open field next to the park. It's been a wonderful addition for the children. Not only do they get to play and meet new friends; they get to enjoy a free and healthy snack.

We walked over, and Sam climbed into the twisting green branches and leaves. "I'm looking for the big red ones. They're in deep," he said as he disappeared further into the thicket.

He emerged with a handful of juicy, ripened red berries and politely told me, "Momma, you can have only two and the rest are for me. That's all the berries we can have today, because we need to share them with the other kids."

Laughing, I popped the two precious berries into my mouth. The bliss of their sweet tang awoke my senses, and all the weariness of the day melted away.

As we walked home later that evening, Sam said, "I hope we come back to the park again tomorrow when you get home from work. I want to eat more raspberries and play again with my friends."

I gently tousled his hair and scooped him into my arms. "We will definitely come back here tomorrow, buddy. Mommy loves eating berries with you."

Allison New
South Portland, Maine

◀ My granddaughter, Ella, loves to visit our farm. She adores the cows and rabbits but shares an extra-special bond with Foxxie.

Chris Redding
Ellsworth, Wisconsin

◀◀ Granddaughter Anika is thrilled to make a new friend while feeding the goats at a local corn maze.

Laurie Smith
*Harrington,
Prince Edward Island*

▼ Brynlee steals a smooch from her barrel horse, Ace.

Rainey Bennett
Hubbard, Texas

▲ Andy sure is proud to drive his Mom-made tractor.

Cindy Shuman
Waldoboro, Maine

My family loves to take scenic drives on the back roads in Brown County, Indiana, and we always slow down to see the old barns. On a sunny afternoon, this curious horse popped out for a visit.

Brady Kesner
Highland, Illinois

Song of Summer

Without a doubt, a screen door slamming is the anthem of summer.

It reminds me of my childhood in Wisconsin, when relatives played cards on our white front porch set between two stately elms.

We kids raced in and out as the screen door, with its old-fashioned fretwork, slammed shut behind us.

Bursts of laughter and the shuffling of cards were tempered only by my father's stern admonishment, "Don't let the screen door slam!" If I close my eyes, I can still hear it.

Like the front door, our back screen door had a lot of character. Unpretentious. Transparent. Inviting. Painted a Granny Smith green, its rickety, mesh-covered wooden frame hung slightly slanted. The rusty hinges creaked when the door opened.

Back in those days, most of the houses had screen doors. Since we didn't have any air conditioning, soft breezes and fresh air blew in through the mesh doors and open windows.

On the inside looking out, I saw purple morning glories and goldfinches at our feeders. I heard bumblebees buzzing and birds singing. I smelled newly cut grass and lavender alongside the house.

Outdoors, a whole world of adventure awaited. We could climb trees. We could ride our bikes to the pool. We could run through a lawn sprinkler. We could play kickball. Oh, what beautiful possibilities!

Linda Schneider
Chilton, Wisconsin

Scrapbook

CAPTURE THE BEAUTY AROUND YOU

Hand-painted with stars and stripes, this rustic barn in Morrill, Maine, watches over the countryside.
Photo by Kevin Shields/Alamy

"After chores in the summer, Grandma put a rocker out on the lawn and we'd watch the stars come out, soon to be followed by the fireflies."

Joan Stratford
Eugene, Oregon

▲ The man in the cowboy hat was so caught up in the show that he moved into my shot.
Laurie Painter
Silver Cliff, Wisconsin

▶ I ran into this little cowboy at the state fair. I visited with him while he practiced his roping and learned all about how involved he is in his family's ranch.
Katherine Plessner
Verona, North Dakota

Ron Trudeau loves taking folks across Lake Weir in his Amphicar, which was built for cruising lakes and rivers (and land). It's quite the head turner.

Lisa Crigar
Ocala, Florida

▲ I took a dream trip out west last summer with my husband, Dan, and our daughter, Ava. This was a beautiful day at Devils Tower in Wyoming, and you can see the contentment on their faces.

Marcia Pedriana
Mukwonago, Wisconsin

▲ Each year, I look forward to seeing the hummingbirds arrive at my home. I plant nectar-rich flowers on my porch to attract them. They are magical creatures!

Sharon Laws
Telford, Tennessee

My grandson, Cale (second from left), and his friends savor a watermelon-eating, seed-spitting, juicy good time in my friend's old Chevrolet truck.

Joan Younger
Sophia, North Carolina

► Anna, one of my sisters, cuddles Luna the cat.

Laura Adrian
Hermosa, South Dakota

▲ My niece Natalie had so much fun picking up and holding her family's new chickens.

Daisy Gangloff
Kokomo, Indiana

► We'd just finished throwing a few bales of hay to the cows when Charlee started crying. To make her happy, her daddy said we could get more cows.

Amber Gordon
Ypsilanti, Michigan

Audrey, my daughter, was hanging out in the field with Mel, my mom's old mare. Mel's a patient babysitter, and the kids all love her.

Sarah Anderson
The Dalles, Oregon

As I admired this patch of smooth oxeye sunflowers, a chatty house wren flew in and perched right on one of the flowers.

Travis Bonovsky
Brooklyn Center, Minnesota

▲ Bison roam the Custer State Park Wildlife Loop.

Laura Adrian
Hermosa, South Dakota

▲ One day while playing golf, I saw movement in the field just off the course. These two fox kits were romping among some railroad ties.

Bonnie Bowne
Fort Collins, Colorado

▶ When a butterfly chooses your garden, it's magical. I grow several flowering plants to attract beauties like this zebra longwing.

Doreen Damm
New Port Richey, Florida

▼ An American robin came to play in the water of a small birdbath on my back deck. It dipped its head in the water and turned around and around.

Mary Jo Mantey
Port Austin, Michigan

My daughter, Trinity, was out petting the cows after the rain passed. She loves playing in the fields with the cattle.

Shaye Cobb
Blairsville, Georgia

> "And God smiled again,
> And the rainbow appeared,
> And curled itself around his shoulder."
>
> **James Weldon Johnson**

▲ Our farm was the pot of gold for this double rainbow. I think our horses were happy to have the weather break.
Cindy Gibson
East Liverpool, Ohio

▶ I took a number of photos after an August thunderstorm, but this is my favorite. It kind of looks as if the rainbow is coming right out of the barn roof.
Dennis Cochran
La Fontaine, Indiana

Grandsons Zander and Tate bask in the warmth from atop a round bale.

Sandy Miller
Byron Center, Michigan

CAITLIN PASMA PHOTOGRAPHY

"I can still hear the rhythmic pounding of the baler punching out bales and smell the aroma of fresh hay. And I thank the good Lord that I was born a farmer's son and raised a country boy."

Dane Schisler
Powell, Ohio

▲ On a visit to a Kansas farm, my grandkids and their friends found a new way to play in the hay. From left are granddaughter Gracie, friend Lauryn, grandson Cooper and friend Madisyn.

Shelly Bell
Sapulpa, Oklahoma

◄ Middlefield is home to the second-largest Amish settlement in our state. On sunny summer days, you'll see farmers making hay along nearly every country back road.

Tami Gingrich
Middlefield, Ohio

► Strong backlighting illuminated Delicate Arch in Utah's Arches National Park.

Bob Oehlman
Irvine, California

▲ During a recent visit to Maine, we came across an artist painting the rocky coast near Pemaquid Point Lighthouse.

Scott Harrell
Glen Allen, Virginia

A flag waves in Chimney Rock
State Park in North Carolina.
Photo by Sean Pavone/Alamy

When my niece Lilly visited the farm, everything was an exciting adventure! She loved wandering down pathways and into the fields.

Kelley Bracken
Rural Retreat, Virginia

▲ As we drove past a sunflower field, my husband couldn't believe it when I wanted to stop to ask the owners if we could photograph their flowers. But, after all, anyone who grows sunflowers must be a wonderful person. The owners welcomed us to photograph there for as long as we wanted. This shot is my favorite.

Denise McQuillan
Fort Wayne, Indiana

◀ My grandsons Aesun and Ethan were filled with joy and patriotic pride on the Fourth of July.

Jim Kucharik
Easton, Pennsylvania

▲ The Meyer clan and a friend make a splash
in the creek at Uncle David's place. Each year,
we meet there for a lazy afternoon.

Joyce Meyer
Spillville, Iowa

I was delighted to see these three
deer crossing an open field at
Yosemite National Park in California.
Alex Hoffman
Johnstown, Pennsylvania

Heart & Soul

FEEL THE LOVE OF COUNTRY

HANDCRAFTED
FURNITURE &
ACCESSORIES

'AN APPEAL TO HEAVEN'

Marie lets the wood guide the type of flag she creates. White-painted wood from a barn in Barrington, Illinois, became a Revolutionary-era Appeal to Heaven flag (left).

Students in Marie's stenciling class expressed interest in purchasing her work, so she turned painting into a profession.

Stars & Stripes Forever

She's 70 now, an age when many folks are starting to eye that comfy recliner in front of the TV. But chances are if there's an old barn coming down anywhere in northeastern Illinois, Marie Roth will be there. Clad in khakis, wearing leather gloves and hefting a circular saw, Marie will pick through the jumble of wood, looking for pieces that, as she describes it, "whisper" to her.

She'll cart off the selected boards to her Long Grove home, where she'll wash them and allow them to air-dry before fitting the pieces together like a puzzle and gluing them into place.

But it's only when she starts painting the assemblage in the bold, beautiful colors beloved by every American that it becomes clear what Marie is creating. From the leftover scraps of broken-down barns, she fashions fine wooden reproductions of the American flag. Ranging from just 18 inches long all the way up to barn door-sized, Marie's flags have a worn, homey quality that strengthens their visual impact and appeal.

"The wood is beautifully aged by animals, humans, sometimes shot with BB's, nailed, hammered, torn, ripped, weathered," she says. "Recently I had wood from a floor that was marked by hooves. I used it to paint flags from the Civil War era—the marks on the wood made me think of all the marching and walking and horse soldiers."

Marie comes by her love of barn wood naturally. Her father was a carpenter, and her grandparents farmed in Iowa. She painted her first flag more than 30 years ago on a shipping pallet she found at a garage sale. The old pallet, she remembers, "just looked like it should be a flag."

A self-taught artist, Marie jokes that she paints these American flags because "I'm real good at drawing straight lines, and that's about it."

She's become a passionate amateur historian of Old Glory's 27 official versions, as well as the famous unofficial ones she paints, including the tattered flag that flew over Fort Sumter when the Union surrendered that battle to the Confederacy at the start of the Civil War.

Each of Marie's works comes with a handwritten note detailing the history of that particular flag. She also tries to connect the wood to her customer, a goal to which fate sometimes lends a hand.

She loves the story of the time she and her daughter collected wood while "running in front of a bulldozer" dismantling an old barn. "Later, a couple contacted me to order a flag," Marie recalls.

"When we met to discuss it, I discovered their new house happened to be on the exact spot where that barn had stood. That brought tears to our eyes."

Don't count on Marie to slow down anytime soon. She's having too much fun—and her flags now fetch between $125 and $1,200.

"Creating art is something I have to do," she says. "I hope I die with a paintbrush in my hand."

Jill Gleeson
State College, Pennsylvania

Strawberry preserves taste sweeter when they're homemade.

Night Shift on the Berry Line

My mother went canning crazy every year. One especially fruitful season back when I was in high school, Mom told me, "The strawberries are ripe at the U-pick, and I expect every one of us to pick our share."

I had other plans, though. I vowed to find a way out. I had sent in my entry for a local tennis tournament that would conflict with Mom's berry madness.

While my mother, aunt and sister scurried about collecting containers, I explained I wouldn't be joining them because of my tennis match. I did my best to act disappointed and promised to lend a hand next season.

My match was grueling. The day was a scorcher, and play did not finish until late evening. Still, I'd won and was scheduled to play in the finals the next morning.

How happy I felt as I made my long walk home from the bus stop. I opened the door and was hit by the heavy, sugar-dank fog found only at an all-out canning fest.

"Looks like you're not going to miss out after all," Mom smiled.

"We picked 88 pounds!" my aunt proudly piped in.

I squeezed past my younger sister, who sat surrounded by berry tubs. She brushed frazzled blond curls from her eyes and kicked a tub toward me. "Start stemming," she said.

I sauntered with my tub to the back porch and began to pull the stems off. Mom had organized the operation like an assembly line, except we were moving fruit, not Fords. My sister and I stemmed a tub and then passed it to my aunt. My aunt washed the berries and then passed them on to Mom, who cooked the preserves and filled the jars. "Keep it moving," she said, as we worked into the night.

I finished my third tub, reached for another and glanced up at the clock. Four hours had passed.

I began to feel some satisfaction. Yes, my hands were stained with strawberry juice, I was hot and tired and my clothes were covered with sticky stems and squished strawberries. But looking at the 50 or so brimful jars of preserves made me happy.

I knew how much those strawberries would mean to us on some frosty fall morning. I knew, too, how satisfied we all were to have put out such effort and gotten so much for it. No store-bought jam would be found in our pantry, because we had preserves that captured our family's fruitfulness. Each jar was an accomplishment. That's why they tasted so good.

Marie Lemond
Kent, Washington

The Art of Gardening

Your garden should tell your story. That rose bush over there? I found it in a postseason closeout at a local nursery. Autumn frost had not yet taken its toll, and the price was right. I saw it and wanted that rose for my garden bed.

That delicate pink rose, mute in contrast to the black-eyed Susan blooming from midsummer until frost, its brown-purple center attracting butterflies and bees to its precious nectar. Yes, easy to grow, casting its lovely, warm color.

Those painted ferns washed with gorgeous silver and burgundy markings brighten the shaded area of the garden. An ancient image, ferns symbolize sincerity and the wisdom of the earth. Their graceful fronds gently unfurl toward the light.

Oh, there are many lessons to be learned in the art of gardening! Working in harmony with nature's cycles, we become more aware of the important relationship between the natural world and ourselves. Gardening is a way of life, developing guidelines for patience, optimism, trust and attention.

The basic principles of gardening are change and growth, patterning our own lives. We learn about the necessity of diversity. We accept the need for forward thinking and long-range planning. At the same time, we learn that we cannot control everything or rush nature's rhythm and timing. We learn to deal with disappointment and to accept an imperfect world.

In return, the garden offers us a quiet place for reflection and contemplation, providing comfort in difficult times. It is a source of tranquility in the fast-paced world we inhabit.

Is there a favorite season in the garden? Is spring the most hopeful time of the year? Not even spring knows if she will be on time. I do know that a garden never dies; it only retreats and sighs. There is a quiet beauty to the garden in winter, sunlight bursting through the cathedral of bare branches. Winter takes us back to the bare essentials, reminding us to appreciate fully what is to come in summer and fall.

Ken Neuser
Green Bay, Wisconsin

Nurturing the land brings its own rewards.

Acres of sunflowers attract guests to Donaldson Farms each summer. At right, million bells, petunias and verbenas bloom at the farm's nursery.

The Sunny Side of Life

From the end of August through the middle of September, I swap my public relations and social media hats for three short, gorgeous, hot but fun-packed weeks of sunflowers. Aided by my loyal and spirited "farmily," I treat guests at Donaldson Farms to stunning views, photo opportunities and fresh-air hayrides.

I never imagined I'd be sharing fascinating facts about sunflowers with so many visitors to the farm where my husband, Greg, grew up. I left the corporate world in 2008, and it's still a treat to have beautiful farmland as an office view and to take my business trips via tractor and wagon.

People of all ages enjoy the farm while our sunflowers are at their most breathtaking. Kids love the Pollinator Safari Hunt that I run. And we offer sunset photography tours and sunflower pick-and-paint events, as well as competitive amateur and professional photo contests. Guests flock to these experiences.

I grew up in the shadow of New York City, where the closest thing to a tractor was a hand-pushed lawn mower. Hackettstown is an hour west of my hometown, yet the scenery is remarkably different.

This place has been in the family since 1906, when Lewis Donaldson traded the deed to his two-bedroom house in the township of West Orange, New Jersey, for what was then about 100 acres of farmland in Hackettstown. Lewis turned the land into a dairy farm.

His great-grandson Lew (my father-in-law) grew up working on that dairy farm, which also included hay,

Homemade tomato sauce, salsa and fresh vegetables line the farm market's shelves.

grain and potato crops. Later, Lew and his wife, Helen, raised their children—Gary, Bob, David, Debbie, Donna and Greg—on the land.

In the 1980s, when Greg was only 14 years old, he convinced his dad to give him a small plot of land where he could grow potatoes and Indian corn. Greg sold his produce from the back of his dad's pickup truck. That little farm stand has become a large and successful retail farm market selling farm-fresh produce, local artisan products and baked goods.

Greg also runs the farm's pick-your-own activities. Thousands of visitors pick our apples, berries and pumpkins each and every year.

My kids, the fifth generation to grow up on the farm, spend their summers collecting lightning bugs, jumping in rain puddles, fighting over who gets to chase basketballs that roll into the horse pasture, and playing among the trees and plants that surround their Uncle David's greenhouse and nursery. They ride their bikes to our farm market for ice cream, and they drive tractors and ride horses, too. Lucky ducks.

Our family farms nearly 1,200 acres throughout Warren County, 500 of which are located on our land. Donaldson Farms also includes a wholesale operation, a nursery and a greenhouse. We grow a large variety of crops, including berries, peaches, perennials, mums, apples, nursery stock, asparagus, tomatoes, peppers, watermelon, garlic, broccoli, lettuce, pumpkins and our famous sunflowers.

This time of year, sunflowers are the stars of our farm. Gary and his son, Justin; Gary's cousin, Jeff; and a large team of farm workers plant 25 acres of sunflowers each

season. The flowers are harvested for birdseed and sunflower oil. Local and migrating birds benefit from the easy-to-crack, soft-shelled black-oil sunflower seeds, which are high in fat. The yellow-hued sunflower oil is a foodie favorite, used in salad dressings and as a dip for fresh crusty bread.

We sell our own sunflower products at farm stands and in small stores throughout the state. A portion of these proceeds directly benefits the New Jersey Audubon Society.

Donaldson's Greenhouse & Nursery is run by David. Early on, David ran this part of Donaldson Farms with his brother, Bob. But the family suffered a tragic loss when Bob passed away from pancreatic cancer in 1999. David has carried on the family's vision and created a stunning business. It features a greenhouse and nursery that offers professional residential and commercial landscaping services. Top-quality annuals, perennials, trees, shrubs, soils and mulches as well as pottery and garden-related items are for sale.

Lew and Helen are still active on the farm. Lew bales hay, and Helen creates seasonal wreaths.

Agritourism activities add value to our business, and they offer great experiences for visitors, who are surprised to learn just how much daily work is needed to maintain and operate a farm.

Season in and season out, I am in awe of my family's work ethic, dedication and passion for doing their part to feed the world. Our children are so fortunate to be raised in this environment.

Katie Donaldson
Hackettstown, New Jersey

Sherry is a lifelong farm girl committed to helping the next generation of farm kids.

Healing the Wounded Spirit

My mother, Sherry Phillips Mitchell, spent her girlhood tagging along with her father, Leslie Edward Phillips, on their southern Ohio farm. She learned how to mend fences, plow fields, make goat cheese and change the oil in the farm's vehicles. And she learned farm life doesn't offer instant rewards, but if you stick with it long enough, the hard work pays off.

My grandpa spent his later years living on a corner of Mom's land, Cherry Ridge Farms, where together they enjoyed a Saturday morning horseback riding ritual until he died in 2011.

Since that time, the farm has blossomed into Cherry Ridge Therapeutic Learning Programs, a center for learning, horseback riding and companionship.

"I am a 'road scholar,' learning in an experiential way," Mom says. She gained programming and fundraising skills while directing a crisis pregnancy center. "I feel I was gifted with eyes to see the needs of a wounded spirit," she adds.

She has partnered with a program called Working to Empower Students Together (WEST), which helps young people who are wrestling with learning disabilities, emotional and behavioral challenges, or unstable home environments. These fifth-through 12th-graders haul hay, muck stalls and ride, groom and halter horses, all guided by Mom's farm rules: No bullying, no swearing and no complaining.

Kids with emotional, physical and mental challenges also get help from her Therapeutic Horsemanship Program, led by instructors certified through PATH, the Professional Association of Therapeutic Horsemanship.

Mom's latest project, the Farm Day Grief Camp, was born out of her own grieving process after the loss of my grandpa. The first session took place in October, and Mom plans to run the camp again this fall.

"I'm an adult woman who lost my dad only six years ago," Mom says. "There is nothing better than nature and animals to help with the grieving process."

The camp's first visitors were five kids mourning the loss of a 7-year-old who died of cancer. Activities included painting memory boxes and recalling the child's favorite things; bonding with Hickory and Misty, the farm's kid-friendly mini horses; and a balloon launch they called Sentiments to Heaven.

"Each camper wrote one thing they wished they could share with their departed loved one on their balloon," Mom says.

Children living with physical disabilities are also welcome at Cherry Ridge Farms. Recently a student in a wheelchair smiled ear to ear as he led Misty and Hickory around the show ring. Mom plans to improve the woodland trail to make it accessible to wheelchairs. And she is creating a monarch sanctuary to facilitate sensory learning.

Mom shares family recipes and stories on her blog, *Take Joy! My Farmhouse Journal*, and in a book of the same name. Her vision inspires children, ensuring that the lessons she has learned on the farm will be preserved for years to come. I know my grandpa would be proud.

Christi Mitchell-Brown
Loveland, Ohio

Competing in rodeos like this one, at Parker Ranch on the Big Island, helps keep DeeDee's skills sharp and her lasso arm steady.

Aloha, Cowgirl!

It's a bright, hot Saturday morning on the dry and rocky slopes of Hualalai, on the Big Island of Hawaii, and DeeDee Keakealani Bertelmann is lifting jagged chunks of lava and carefully moving them back in place. The lava rocks form walls, many of them built by her great-great-great-grandfather and his brothers, and these walls have been corralling cattle for generations. Some are more than 200 years old.

As the fifth generation in a family of *paniolo*, or Hawaiian cowboys, DeeDee would rather spend the day riding horses. But more often than not, weekends find her and her family checking and fixing the miles of rock walls that crisscross their ancestral land. The family still traverses much of the ranch on horseback, because many areas are too rocky to be accessible by an all-terrain vehicle. "I always wanted to be a cowboy when I grew up," she says. "When that's all you know, it's kind of hard to do anything else."

Her family raises around 200 crossbred Angus cattle on 1,000 acres leased from the state. DeeDee's RK Livestock ranch is on just a portion of the original Pu'uwa'awa'a Ranch, which spread from the mountains to the sea and

DeeDee and her family speak Hawaiian when they're rounding up *pipi*, the word for cattle (above). Horses are family, too, but Dually, a favorite, gets extra affection from DeeDee (left).

was first leased out by the government of Hawaii in 1892. Now a calf-cow operation, the ranch sends most of its weanlings to feedlots on the U.S. mainland. DeeDee's relatives also fish, hunt wild pigs, raise chickens, grow vegetables and gather crab and limpets.

Oral histories passed from generation to generation link DeeDee's ancestors to this area long before Hawaii began leasing the land to them. "When we're on the land, it's almost an intimate relationship because of the connection between our family and the '*āina*," or land, she says.

Visitors are more likely to associate the Hawaiian landscape with sun and surf, and few probably realize the paniolo were wrangling cattle in the islands' rugged uplands and lush forests decades before cowboys started riding the range in the American West. Mexican *vaqueros* were brought to Hawaii around 1830 to teach Native Hawaiians how to tame the cattle running wild after being brought to the islands in 1793.

The paniolo worked ranches across the Hawaiian Islands. The first significant one, Parker Ranch, was founded on the Big Island in 1847 and, along with other ranches like Pu'uwa'awa'a, served as the islands' main source of beef through the 1960s.

Today, while only a handful of commercial cattle operations remain, many islanders practice traditional skills through rodeo and their work on family ranches like DeeDee's. She and her husband plan to retain their state leases and keep the ranch going.

"We will do everything in our power to give our children and our grandchildren the opportunity to be on our ancestral lands," she says.

Like many Native Hawaiians who lost ancestral land, DeeDee describes a heaviness in knowing these areas once belonged to them. But she finds a sense of connection in continuing the traditions of her ancestors.

"I always wonder if what I'm doing today meets my ancestors' approval," she says. "It means even more when they can see my daughters and my nieces and my grandson living off the land."

Ilima Loomis
Haiku, Hawaii

The Lake Effect

Every kid needs an adventure or two in the summer.

In the early 1950s, our dad bought a small parcel of land in Edinburg, New York, in the Adirondack Mountains near the Great Sacandaga Lake. During those early days we camped in an old city passenger bus Dad had purchased and gutted down to an empty shell.

Little by little (and on a shoestring budget), Dad transformed the bus into what would become our home away from home for many years. In the evenings, before electricity was installed, we sat by the light of kerosene lamps and kept warm with a potbelly stove. We brought water in gallon jugs from our home in the city and kept food cold in an old icebox.

Later, Dad added a kitchen and bathroom, a living room with a fireplace, a guest room and a small area for his workshop. Eventually we joined the modern world with electricity and a dug well.

On any given warm summer day, my sister Barbara, friends Elliott and Aleta and cousins Janice and Joyce always found something to occupy our time. Every day was an adventure—we didn't know what it was like to be bored.

Sometimes we'd trek up the hill behind our camps with lunches packed in brown paper bags and find a cool, mossy area to sit and have a picnic. From that vantage point, we could look out and see sailboats on the lake and motorboats towing water skiers.

During blackberry season, each of us would grab a large pan and pick as many berries as it would hold so that our moms could make blackberry jelly. We often returned to camp with purple stains on our fingers, many mosquito bites and blackberry-thorn scratches crisscrossing our legs.

With our parents' permission and a dime in our pockets, we sometimes walked to the small general store to treat ourselves to penny candy, a Popsicle or a cold bottle of soda.

On many evenings we'd build a fire and toast marshmallows until they were flaming torches. Quite a few ended up in the fire and not in our mouths. Our hands and faces were gooey, sticky messes, but it never bothered us. Away from city lights, the evening sky was lit with countless stars, and we'd gaze up to see who could find the Big and Little dippers. Whip-poor-wills serenaded us, a sound I still love.

On days when Dad wasn't too busy working on the camp, we'd pile in the car with a thermos of lemonade, a cooler with hot dogs and rolls, and our beach towels. What a treat it was to swim in the lake and roast hot dogs over a fire.

At the time, I don't think we appreciated how fortunate we were to have a summer getaway, to play in the fresh clear air and cool off in the lake waters. Now, as an adult in my 60s, I look back and treasure those memories of an adventurous, joyful, wonderful childhood. We were truly blessed.

Christine Saglimbeni
Schenectady, New York

Barbara (front), Christine (left), Elliot and Aleta bonded at the lake.

A Taste of Summer

SAVOR THE FLAVORS OF THE SEASON

Grilled Sweet Corn

PREP: 10 MIN. + SOAKING • **GRILL:** 25 MIN. • **MAKES:** 8 SERVINGS

INGREDIENTS

- 8 large ears sweet corn in husks
- 6 tablespoons butter, softened
- 1 tablespoon minced fresh parsley
- 1 to 2 teaspoons chili powder
- 1 teaspoon garlic salt
- ½ to 1 teaspoon ground cumin

DIRECTIONS

1. Place corn in a stockpot; cover with cold water. Soak 20 minutes.
2. Mix remaining ingredients. Drain corn; carefully peel back husks to within 1 in. of bottoms and remove silk. Spread corn with butter mixture; rewrap in husks and secure with kitchen string.
3. Grill corn, covered, over medium heat until tender, 25-30 minutes, turning often. To serve, cut string and peel back husks.

Grilled Sweet Onions

PREP: 15 MIN. • **GRILL:** 35 MIN.
MAKES: 4 SERVINGS

INGREDIENTS
- 4 large sweet onions
- 4 teaspoons beef bouillon granules
- 1½ teaspoons minced fresh thyme or
  ½ teaspoon dried thyme
- ¼ teaspoon salt
- ¼ teaspoon pepper
- 4 tablespoons butter
- 4 teaspoons white wine or beef broth, optional

DIRECTIONS
1. Prepare grill for indirect heat. Peel onions, leaving root ends intact. Cut a thin slice from the top of each, then carefully cut a 1-in. hole in the center. Cut each onion into quarters, cutting to within ½ in. of bottom. Place each onion on a double thickness of heavy-duty foil (about 12 in. square).
2. Sprinkle bouillon, thyme, salt and pepper into centers; top with butter. If desired, drizzle with wine. Fold foil around onions, sealing tightly.
3. Grill onions, covered, over indirect medium heat until tender, 35-40 minutes. Open foil carefully to allow steam to escape.

Strawberry Corn Salsa

PREP: 15 MIN. + CHILLING
MAKES: 5½ CUPS

INGREDIENTS
- 2 cups fresh strawberries, chopped
- 2 cups grape tomatoes, chopped
- 1 package (10 ounces) frozen corn, thawed
- 2 green onions, chopped
- 3 tablespoons minced fresh cilantro
- ⅓ cup olive oil
- 2 tablespoons raspberry vinegar
- 2 tablespoons lime juice
- ½ teaspoon salt
  Baked tortilla chips

DIRECTIONS
In a large bowl, combine the first five ingredients. In a small bowl, whisk the oil, vinegar, lime juice and salt. Drizzle over strawberry mixture; toss to coat. Refrigerate for 1 hour. Serve with chips.

Oven-Fried Chicken Drumsticks

PREP: 20 MIN. + MARINATING • **BAKE:** 40 MIN.
MAKES: 4 SERVINGS

INGREDIENTS

- 1 cup fat-free plain Greek yogurt
- 1 tablespoon Dijon mustard
- 2 garlic cloves, minced
- 8 chicken drumsticks (4 ounces each), skin removed
- ½ cup whole wheat flour
- 1½ teaspoons paprika
- 1 teaspoon baking powder
- 1 teaspoon salt
- 1 teaspoon pepper
  Olive oil-flavored cooking spray

DIRECTIONS

1. In a large resealable plastic bag, combine yogurt, mustard and garlic. Add chicken; seal bag and turn to coat. Refrigerate 8 hours or overnight.
2. Preheat oven to 425°. In another plastic bag, mix flour, paprika, baking powder, salt and pepper. Remove the chicken from marinade and add, one piece at a time, to flour mixture; close bag and shake to coat. Place on a wire rack over a baking sheet; spritz with cooking spray. Bake 40-45 minutes or until a thermometer reads 165°.

Sweet & Tangy Freezer Pickles

PREP: 20 MIN. + CHILLING • **COOK:** 5 MIN. + FREEZING
MAKES: 32 SERVINGS (¼ CUP EACH)

INGREDIENTS

- 2 pounds pickling cucumbers (about 8 to 10 medium), trimmed and thinly sliced
- 3 medium onions, thinly sliced
- 1 large green pepper, chopped
- 3 tablespoons salt, divided
- 2 cups sugar
- 1 cup white vinegar
- 3 teaspoons celery seed

DIRECTIONS

1. In a large glass or stainless steel bowl, toss vegetables with 2 tablespoons salt. Cover with crushed ice and mix well. Refrigerate, covered, 8 hours. Drain and rinse; drain mixture well. Return to bowl.
2. In a saucepan, combine sugar, vinegar, celery seed and remaining salt. Bring to a boil; cook and stir 1 minute. Pour over cucumber mixture; stir to combine.
3. Transfer to freezer containers or canning jars, leaving 1-in. headspace; cool completely. Freeze, covered, up to 6 months.
4. Thaw in refrigerator before serving. Store thawed pickles in the refrigerator up to 2 weeks.

Patchwork Quilt Cake

PREP: 55 MIN. • **BAKE:** 40 MIN. + COOLING
MAKES: 15 SERVINGS

INGREDIENTS

- ⅔ cup butter, softened
- 1¾ cups sugar
- 1 tablespoon vanilla extract
- 2 large eggs
- 2½ cups all-purpose flour
- 2½ teaspoons baking powder
- ½ teaspoon salt
- 1¼ cups 2% milk

FROSTING

- 1 cup butter, softened
- 3 cups confectioners' sugar
- 4 teaspoons vanilla extract
- 3 to 4 tablespoons heavy whipping cream
  Assorted fresh berries

DIRECTIONS

1. Preheat oven to 350°. Grease a 13x9-in. baking dish.

2. Cream butter and sugar until light and fluffy. Add vanilla and eggs, one at a time, beating well. In another bowl, whisk together flour, baking powder and salt; beat into creamed mixture alternately with milk. Transfer to prepared dish.

3. Bake until a toothpick inserted in the center comes out clean, 40-45 minutes. Place on a wire rack; cool completely.

4. For frosting, beat butter until creamy; gradually beat in confectioners' sugar until smooth and light in color, about 3 minutes. Beat in vanilla and 3 tablespoons cream until light and fluffy, about 2 minutes; thin with additional cream if desired. Spread over cake. Before serving, top with berries in a patchwork quilt pattern.

Calgary Stampede Ribs

PREP: 2¼ HOURS + MARINATING • **GRILL:** 15 MIN.
MAKES: 8 SERVINGS

INGREDIENTS

- 4 pounds pork baby back ribs, cut into serving-size pieces
- 3 garlic cloves, minced
- 1 tablespoon sugar
- 2 teaspoons salt
- 1 tablespoon paprika
- 2 teaspoons ground cumin
- 2 teaspoons chili powder
- 2 teaspoons pepper

BARBECUE SAUCE
- 2 tablespoons butter
- 1 small onion, finely chopped
- 1 cup ketchup
- ¼ cup packed brown sugar
- 3 tablespoons lemon juice
- 3 tablespoons Worcestershire sauce
- 2 tablespoons cider vinegar
- 1½ teaspoons ground mustard
- 1 teaspoon celery seed
- ⅛ teaspoon cayenne pepper

DIRECTIONS

1. Preheat oven to 325°. Rub ribs with garlic; place in a roasting pan. Bake, covered, until tender, about 2 hours.
2. Mix sugar, salt and spices; sprinkle over ribs. Remove from pan; cool slightly. Refrigerate, covered, 8 hours or overnight.
3. In a small saucepan, heat butter over medium heat; saute onion until tender. Stir in remaining ingredients; bring to a boil. Reduce heat; cook, uncovered, until thickened, about 10 minutes, stirring frequently.
4. Brush ribs with some of the sauce. Grill, covered, over medium heat until heated through, 12-15 minutes, turning and brushing occasionally with additional sauce. Serve with remaining sauce.

Curried Chicken & Peach Salad

START TO FINISH: 10 MIN. • **MAKES:** 4 SERVINGS

INGREDIENTS

- ½ cup fat-free mayonnaise
- 1 teaspoon curry powder
- 2 cups cubed cooked chicken breasts
- ½ cup chopped walnuts
- ¼ cup raisins
- 2 medium peaches, sliced
- 1 package (5 ounces) spring mix salad greens

DIRECTIONS

Mix mayonnaise and curry powder; toss gently with chicken, walnuts and raisins. Serve chicken mixture and peaches over greens.

Grilled Garden Pizza

START TO FINISH: 30 MIN.
MAKES: 6 SERVINGS

INGREDIENTS

- 2 plum tomatoes, thinly sliced
- ½ teaspoon sea salt or kosher salt
- 1 loaf (1 pound) frozen pizza dough, thawed
- 2 tablespoons olive oil, divided
- ½ cup shredded Parmesan or Asiago cheese
- ½ cup fresh or frozen corn, thawed
- ¼ cup thinly sliced red onion
- 8 ounces fresh mozzarella cheese, sliced
- ½ cup thinly sliced fresh spinach
- 3 tablespoons chopped fresh basil

DIRECTIONS

1. Sprinkle tomatoes with salt; set aside. On a lightly floured surface, divide dough in half. Roll or press each to ¼-in. thickness; place each on a greased sheet of foil (about 10 in. square). Brush tops with 1 tablespoon oil.
2. Carefully invert crusts onto grill rack, removing foil. Brush tops with remaining oil. Grill, covered, over medium heat 2-3 minutes or until bottom is golden brown. Remove from grill; reduce grill temperature to low.
3. Top grilled sides of crusts with Parmesan or Asiago cheese, tomatoes, corn, onion and mozzarella cheese. Grill, covered, on low heat 4-6 minutes or until cheese is melted. Sprinkle with spinach and basil.

Chicken Salad Croissants

START TO FINISH: 15 MIN.
MAKES: 6 SERVINGS

INGREDIENTS

- ⅔ cup mayonnaise
- ½ cup dill pickle relish
- 1 tablespoon minced fresh parsley
- 1 teaspoon lemon juice
- ½ teaspoon seasoned salt
- ⅛ teaspoon pepper
- 2 cups cubed cooked chicken
- 1 cup cubed Swiss cheese
- 6 croissants, split
  Lettuce leaves

DIRECTIONS

Mix first six ingredients; stir in chicken and cheese. Serve on croissants lined with lettuce.

Juicy Cherry Pie

PREP: 35 MIN. + CHILLING • **BAKE:** 55 MIN. + COOLING • **MAKES:** 8 SERVINGS

INGREDIENTS

- 2½ cups all-purpose flour
- ½ teaspoon salt
- ⅔ cup cold unsalted butter, cubed
- ⅓ cup shortening
- 6 to 10 tablespoons ice water

FILLING

- 5 cups fresh tart cherries, pitted
- 2 teaspoons lemon juice
- ¼ teaspoon almond extract
- 1 cup sugar
- ⅓ cup all-purpose flour
- 1 teaspoon ground cinnamon

SUGAR TOPPING

- 1 tablespoon 2% milk
- 1 teaspoon sugar

DIRECTIONS

1. In a large bowl, mix flour and salt; cut in butter and shortening until crumbly. Gradually add ice water, tossing with a fork until dough holds together when pressed. Divide the dough in half. Shape each into a disk; wrap in plastic. Refrigerate for 1 hour or overnight.

2. Preheat oven to 375°. For filling, place cherries in a large bowl; drizzle with lemon juice and almond extract. In a small bowl, mix sugar, flour and cinnamon. Sprinkle over cherries and toss gently to coat.

3. On a lightly floured surface, roll one half of dough to a ⅛-in.-thick circle; transfer to a 9-in. pie plate. Trim pastry even with rim. Add filling.

4. Roll remaining dough to a ⅛-in.-thick circle; cut out stars or other shapes using cookie cutters. Place top pastry over the filling. Trim, seal and flute edge. If desired, decorate top with cutouts.

5. Bake 40 minutes. For topping, brush top of pie with milk; sprinkle with sugar. Bake 15-20 minutes longer or until crust is golden brown and filling is bubbly. Cool on a wire rack.

Handcrafted with Love

CREATE A FEELING OF HOME

Stick 'Em Up

Household notes will stay put on a washboard memo station that doubles as a handy cupboard.

WHAT YOU'LL NEED
- **Washboard with metal corrugated section**
- **¾-in. wood, 3½ in. wide and 8½ ft. long**
- **Particleboard**
- **2 hinges**
- **Small cabinet doorknob**
- **Nails and screws**
- **Drill**
- **Nail gun or hammer**
- **Wood stain, optional**
- **Foam brushes or rag, optional**

DIRECTIONS

1. Measure washboard from bottom of legs to about an inch from the top. Cut two pieces of the ¾-in. wood to that length for the sides of the cupboard.

2. Measure the width of the washboard. Cut two pieces of ¾-in. wood to that length minus 1½ in. for the top and bottom of the cupboard.

3. Nail the two sides, top and bottom together to create a box frame.

4. Cut the desired number of shelves from the remaining ¾-in. wood, using the length of the top and bottom pieces as a guide. Nail the shelf pieces into place in the box.

5. Measure the height and width of the box frame and cut a piece of particleboard to fit. Nail the particleboard to the back of the box frame.

6. Stain the box to match the washboard finish, if desired.

7. Place washboard on top of the box and determine where the hinges best fit. Drill pilot holes and screw the hinges in place on the box and the washboard.

8. Screw the doorknob onto the leg of the washboard opposite the hinges.

9. Hang cupboard on the wall and place magnets on the metal washboard.

Wish You Were Here

A secondhand picture frame squares up travel memories from generations past.

WHAT YOU'LL NEED

- Empty picture frame
- Interior spray paint
- Twine
- Flat-head thumbtacks
- Medium-grit sandpaper
- Clothespins

DIRECTIONS

1. Lightly sand the picture frame. Apply two coats of paint to frame, allowing it to dry between coats.

2. Cut lengths of twine slightly wider than the frame. Tie knots in each end and hammer thumbtacks through the knots on the back of the frame. Space the twine so there is enough room to hang cards in each row. Trim the ends of the twine.

3. Hang the frame on a wall. Use clothespins to attach postcards along the lengths of twine.

You Dirty Dog

Muddy paws? Keep everything you need at the ready with a handy dog-washing spot that really cleans up.

WHAT YOU'LL NEED

- Galvanized washtub
- Distressed wood
- Screws
- Hook
- Circular saw
- Drill with a metal drill bit

DIRECTIONS

1. Measure the interior width of the washtub where the shelf will be placed. Cut the piece of wood to that length.

2. Drill two holes on each side of the washtub at the point where the shelf will sit. Align the shelf inside. Drive screws through the washtub into the wood, securing it in place.

3. Drill a hole in the bottom of the washtub to align with the hook. Screw the hook into place.

4. Drill two holes in the bottom of the washtub. Hang the tub near an exterior faucet using screws driven through the holes. Drape a hose around the outside and attach to the faucet.

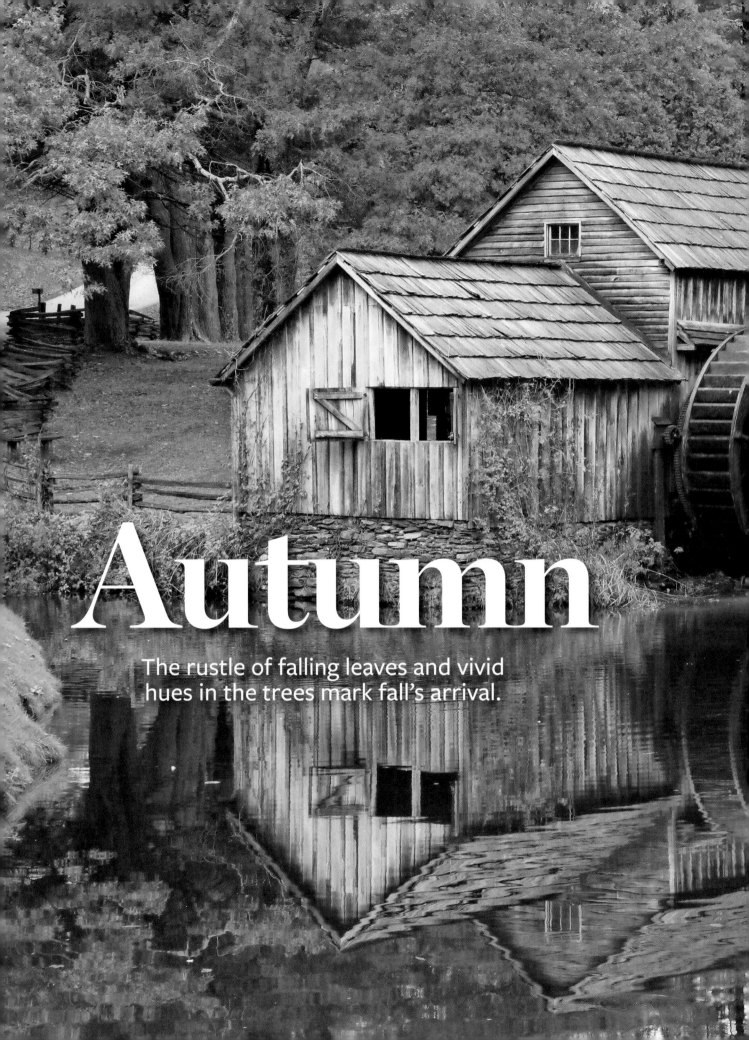

Autumn

The rustle of falling leaves and vivid
hues in the trees mark fall's arrival.

Mabry Mill in Virginia invites
visitors to explore the past.
Photo by Pat & Chuck Blackley

The Good Life

APPRECIATE THE SIMPLE PLEASURES

Fall foliage adorns the hills around Cloudland Farm in Vermont.

Silver Linings

Cloudland Farm has been in my husband's family since his grandfather bought the property in 1908. It was originally a dairy farm that also sold Berkshire pork and had a sawmill. Butter made on the farm was shipped to Boston by rail.

The farm transitioned from dairy to beef cattle in the 1960s. My husband, Bill, took over management of the farm in the late '70s. He grew up in the big house on top of the hill with his father, mother and sister. He then moved into the farm manager's house, built in the '50s down by the livestock barn, when he started running the place.

I came to work on the farm in the late '80s, and the rest is history. Our three children, twins Abby and Meg, 22, and Will, 20, have grown up working on the farm with us. Abby just graduated from college in May and will work as a registered nurse in Virginia.

Meg graduates this coming year with a degree in ecological agriculture and is working with a local landscaping company for the summer. Will has two more years of college before he completes his degree in construction management. Everyone pitches in around the farm wherever they are needed.

Bill also has a son, Nat, from a previous marriage. Nat is married to Molly and lives in Peacham, Vermont, with their two daughters, Elizabeth and Elsie. They are just starting their own vegetable farm there.

Today Cloudland Farm is a little more than 1,000 acres, located 4 miles up a dirt road. Much of the land is forested and is a certified tree farm. The development rights were donated to the Vermont Land Trust to ensure that the farm would remain mostly undeveloped in the future.

The Appalachian Trail corridor runs right through our property, and hikers frequent the farm store during the long, humid summer months.

The oldest portion of the big house dates back to 1795, and it was the first meetinghouse in Pomfret. Over the past three years, Bill and I remodeled the house to make it more energy efficient—with a new roof, windows, insulation and siding—and plan to move into it in the near future.

Bill manages the land, rotational grazing and care of livestock, including Black Angus cattle, pigs and pastured poultry. He also is in charge of clipping pastures, maintaining fences, making hay and maintaining the machinery. He makes haylage bales, dry round bales and small square bales for winter livestock feed and a small amount to sell. An outdoor wood boiler heats the farmhouse and restaurant, so he also spends many days cutting firewood.

I do all of the bookkeeping, and I help Bill with spring and fall cattle roundups for weaning, deworming and vaccinating. I also plant and maintain two vegetable gardens for the family and our restaurant.

The post-and-beam restaurant building, designed by a friend who once worked on the farm, was completed in 2010. The posts, beams, trim and wainscoting on

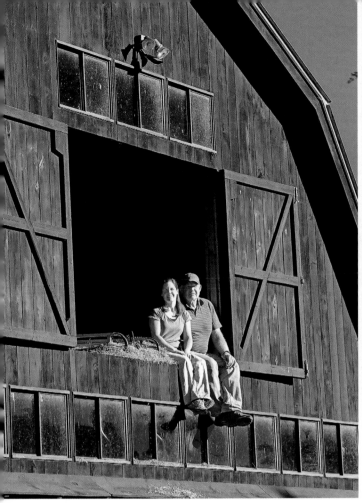

In addition to raising cattle, Cathy and Bill (left) also run a restaurant on the farm. Above: Cathy cuts flowers to decorate the dining tables.

the walls are made of eastern white pine that was harvested off the farm. Restaurant guests enjoy sitting on the porch when the weather is warm and seeing the beautiful view down the valley into Woodstock.

The restaurant seats 50 people, by reservation only. We serve three-course dinners on Thursdays, Fridays and Saturdays from late June through October, and on Fridays and Saturdays during the other seasons. We close in March during "mud season." All the meats we serve and flowers on the tables are raised right here at the farm. We also grow many of the vegetables and herbs and some of the fruit we serve. The other ingredients are sourced from local Vermont farmers. Menus are posted on our website on Wednesday mornings. Dining here is truly a farm-to-table experience.

Ira White is our full-time chef. He makes everything from scratch. We have a staff of about nine part-time restaurant employees during the summer. I manage the restaurant and work almost every night as the hostess. This makes for some long days, but it is very rewarding to see folks enjoying the fruits of our family's labor.

We also have a farm store in our restaurant building where we sell retail cuts of our natural Angus beef, pork cuts, beef and pork sausages, eggs, pickles, beef jerky, and a few other local Vermont products such as maple syrup, sodas, ice cream and cheeses.

We no longer board horses on the farm, but we still keep two retired horses that Meg and Abby grew up

with. We also have a small flock of free-range laying hens and 13 growing Berkshire piglets that were born on the farm this spring. Two of them will be kept as replacement gilts for breeding, and the remainder will be processed for pork.

We process about 125 meat chickens each year for the restaurant, and we raise 40 to 50 turkeys for Thanksgiving. Thankfully, our three barn cats keep the mouse population down. The number of Black Angus cattle fluctuates throughout the year. Currently, we have about 115 head.

Our 1-acre pond is one of our favorite places on the farm. It is very peaceful, with a hayfield on one side and pastures on the other. Often we'll see deer or wild turkeys there.

Fall is spectacular, with brilliantly colored hardwoods covering every hillside. Fall is also apple cider time. We have an old press and enjoy gathering family and friends for a special cider-making party.

Cloudland Farm is a very peaceful place. It's usually quiet, with the exception of the birds singing and an occasional cow mooing. We are truly in God's country; it feels very close to heaven here. The combination of open pastures and hayfields and vast forests makes it a very beautiful place to live or visit.

Cathy Emmons
North Pomfret, Vermont

▼ My lovely daughter Kinsey-Rose shares a special moment with her 9-month-old Friesian colt, Titan.

Susan Frazier
Lebanon, Tennessee

▲ It always pays to have a camera with you when you walk. This farm is along the Ma and Pa Trail in Harford County.

Steve Edwards
Joppa, Maryland

Dear Ol' Dad's Sweater

It is late October, and it is time to rake the leaves. I usually wait for all the leaves to fall so I don't have to do the job twice.

On this crisp, cloudless morning, I'm wearing sweatpants, a flannel shirt and a gold-colored sweater. Once fashionable, the sweater is now faded and stained, has a hole in the left elbow and a wide, soiled collar, and it is missing all five buttons.

The sweater belonged to my dad. I had given it to him new on a Christmas long ago. It saw a lot of holidays and events over the years, but eventually the sweater frayed badly and was relegated to leaf-raking and other yard work. When I cleaned out Dad's hall closet after he died, I found it.

"Are you going to throw this gold sweater in the rag bag?" my wife, Carole, asked me after giving it the once-over.

"No way," I protested. "It's special."

When I wear it now to gather the leaves, my dad feels close. I can faintly smell his Old Spice cologne on the fabric. I feel his warmth, his strength. I see him making a humongous pile of leaves for the grandkids to cannonball into. It seems when I wear the sweater, I rake up as many memories as leaves.

Our acreage in northwestern New Jersey is surrounded by hardwood trees. Pear and apple trees flank the western end of the lawn, while in the center stand two dwarf crab apple trees. There are leaves galore.

Dad said to always have a plan, so I start raking at the house and work my way toward the road. I am a little rusty but soon develop a cadence. My heart pumps and my muscles flex as the carpet of colorful leaves gradually retreats.

When I approach the crab apple trees, squirrels scatter from polishing off the rest of the marble-size fruit. It has been a banner year, and Carole and I put up 10 jars of tangy crab apple jelly—Dad's all-time favorite sweet. He loved spreading it on toasted English muffins. Carole says I definitely inherited my sweet tooth from him.

I survey my progress. I'm almost to Carole's rose garden. Virtually all the hybrid tea roses have ceased blooming except for one ready-to-open John F. Kennedy. Dad gave Carole the white rose for Mother's Day one year.

Suddenly, something bright yellow catches my eye. "Well, I'll be," I exclaim. It's a dandelion flower in full bloom in late October! That's like finding a four-leaf clover, sure to bring good luck, Dad once told me. In April, hundreds, maybe thousands dot the lawn. Dad and I always said that one spring we were going to harvest the flowers and brew dandelion wine. Sadly, we never got the chance before he passed away.

I reach the road, collect the mail and return to the house. "Finished raking?" Carole asks as she plucks an errant leaf from my sweater's collar.

"Yep, all done."

"You know, you look just like your dad in that sweater," Carole says.

And that's one of the nicest things Carole—or for that matter anyone else—has ever said to me.

George M. Flynn
Newton, New Jersey

We saw this red fox at Blackhawk Lodges in Estes Park, Colorado, a place where we have vacationed for 20-plus years. With that sad little face, what better name than Hobo?

Butch Burkhardt
Richmond, Indiana

My great-niece, Lorelei has learned patience from walking with her curious dog.

Barbara Niewenhuis
Grand Rapids, Michigan

When Sidney-Lynn offered to help me in the yard, I suggested that we rake leaves. Of course, it wasn't all work—we had to make time for play!

Cynthia Hodges
Havana, Kansas

The Peaceable Kingdom

Cally, our calico cat adopted from close friends, was quite elderly and fading fast. Winter is a tough time for barn cats, even with snug shelter, plentiful food and water. She spent her days and nights in a nest of hay on the floor of our horse barn. I brought her a rug to give her more cushion and protection from drafts, and I was not surprised to find her permanently curled up there one morning.

When Cally first arrived on our farm, our aging dog Tango initially approached her somewhat warily, given the reaction Tango elicited from our other cats (typically a hiss, scratch and spit). Instead, Cally marched right up and rubbed noses with Tango, and they became fast friends, cuddling together whenever it was time to take a nap. Tango loved anyone who would snuggle up to her, and Cally was the perfect belly warmer. In no time, she became the undisputed leader of the farm.

Our free-range Araucana rooster, however, seemed to seriously question this dog-and-cat relationship. He was indignant about the communal nap time and would strut up the sidewalk, walk up and down the porch and perch on the railing, muttering about how improper it was, at times getting quite loud. They ignored him, which *really* bugged him, proud bird that he was.

One fall morning, as I opened the front door to get the newspaper, I was astonished to see not just a cat and dog snuggled together on the porch, but the rooster as well, tucked up next to Tango's tail. As usual, Tango and Cally didn't move a muscle when I appeared.

The rooster, however, was startled to see me, almost embarrassed. He stood up quickly, flapped his wings, and swaggered off crowing.

No, I didn't have my camera and I never found them all together ever again. You, dear reader, will just have to take it on faith.

I figure a dog, a cat and a rooster sleeping together was our farm's version of the lion and lamb lying down together. The peaceable kingdom was right outside our door, a harbinger of what is promised someday for the rest of us. Despite claws, teeth and talons, it will be possible to snuggle in harmony.

Our special Cally made it happen on earth. I suspect she's met up with Tango, and possibly one rooster, for a nice nap on the other side.

Emily Gibson
Everson, Washington

▲ An early-morning rainbow appears at the Towers of the Virgin in Utah.

Photo by Tim Fitzharris

◄ A dramatic dawn sky over scenic Highway 7 rewards early risers in Arkansas.

Photo by Paul Caldwell

Me, Preston, Ella, Bronwyn and Phillip

Thanksgiving at Bear Creek

For many people, Thanksgiving conjures images of hearth and home, massive turkeys roasting in ovens, mountains of dressing and rivers of warm, rich gravy. For my family, however, it evokes images of a cabin on Lookout Mountain in Alabama.

Until a few years ago, Thanksgiving was one of those holidays we'd allowed to slip through the cracks. That's when my wife and I decided it was high time to make our own family tradition, tucked away in a cabin.

After a quick Internet search, we headed east toward Fort Payne, Alabama. Our destination was Bear Creek Log Cabins. Our plan was to spend the long holiday weekend with our four youngest children and stay completely unplugged from the world.

We wanted our time there to be relaxing: preparing simple meals, playing board and card games, roaming the big woods, roasting marshmallows to make s'mores. In short, we wanted to make memories with each other that would last a lifetime.

We were in for a real treat.

After a long and winding drive up Lookout Mountain, arriving at Bear Creek was like going back in time. The property was anchored by a quaint farmhouse flanked by a gentle swell of open, green pastures, a pond just big enough for fishing, and wooded hills filled with pine and scattered hardwoods. Behind the farmhouse lay an unusual site: a stand of hardwoods filled with irregularly shaped, mammoth-sized boulders—some far larger than a two-story house—that were cast about like some giant's forgotten playthings. The property owners' goats climbed and cavorted among these huge rocks, enjoying their own private paradise.

Brannon and his family left behind the noise of city life to spend Thanksgiving in a cabin talking around a campfire, playing games and befriending goats (above).

Inside, the cabins were just as one would imagine: wrought iron framed beds, open lofts, handmade cabinetry and comfortably worn barn-wood tables and carved chairs. All in all, it was the perfect place for our intended mission.

The next few days flew by. We would talk, laugh, roam the hills and hollows, pet and feed the cows and goats, fish at the pond, play hide-and-seek and capture the flag amid the boulder field, sit around the campfire, sing songs, gaze at the stars and more.

We soon discovered that our cabin backed up to the well-known Little River Canyon National Preserve, and we climbed down and spent nearly a day exploring the canyon floor. A short drive away, the breathtaking DeSoto Falls awaited, followed by homemade ice cream cones gleefully eaten, despite the cold wind outside.

Before we knew it, our children were having so much fun outside that they didn't miss the things they'd left behind. There were no calls for TV, computers or video games. Our kids were filled with wonder and laughter, thoroughly enjoying their time outside, creating games purely from their imaginations and what was on hand. When darkness fell, out came the crafts and the games.

Sitting around the table, we put together a gingerbread house and fashioned handmade ornaments for our Christmas tree. We played endless rounds of Uno and Phase 10, and we made memories.

Our Thanksgiving meal included our family favorites: a honey ham, mashed potatoes from scratch, rolls and green beans. The focus was on family, not fancy, and it was a glorious meal. Afterward, everyone gathered, snuggling together around the crackling fire pit, and we began a tradition that continues to this day: From youngest to oldest, we all took turns sharing the things we were thankful for. Truth be told, these moments are the most precious ones of the trip.

It was a Thanksgiving unlike any other, and long before it was time to head home, we'd decided that next year, Lord willing, we would return to Bear Creek, and we did. Now our Thanksgiving tradition has grown to include our entire extended family. Last year, 33 of us descended upon our own little slice of heaven on earth for a Thanksgiving tradition that will echo for many years to come.

Brannon Hollingsworth
Hartselle, Alabama

Scrapbook

CAPTURE THE BEAUTY AROUND YOU

The vibrancy of fall abounds in this lovely scene of Sugarcreek in Holmes County, Ohio.
Photo by Doyle Yoder

"I love everything about fall—from the way the crisp morning air kisses your nose to the feel of a warm fire heating your toes."

Deborah Moe
Culver, Minnesota

▲ Gathering food for winter is top priority for this pika in Yellowstone National Park.
Photo by Diana LeVasseur

▶ The Merced River flows toward El Capitan in California's Yosemite National Park.
Photo by Mary Liz Austin

Fiery vine maples stand in crimson contrast to the dark green forests of Mount Hood.
Photo by Larry Geddis

▲ This adorable little farmer takes a rest after playing in a big corn maze near South Bend, Indiana.

David Path
Nicholasville, Kentucky

▲ It was so refreshing to watch these two young burrowing owls protect one another. A few moments before this shot, they were beak kissing.

Mary-Ann Ingrao
Angola, New York

Rio Grande Gorge must have
startled early explorers who
happened upon it.
Photo by Adam Schallau

"I appreciate Thanksgiving more and more as I get older. It's a time to stop and give thanks for all we have. It's a time to teach our children about gratitude and to be with family."

Stacie Rogers *Bloomfield, New York*

My daughter and I take nature walks in a nearby park where monarchs gather.
Deb Jencks
Coventry, Rhode Island

▲ I often sit and soak in the season on this cozy swing in my front yard.
Mary Ellen Bergbower
Newton, Illinois

▶ The delights of harvest season—apples, squash and mums—welcome visitors to the charming Vermont Country Store in Weston.
Photo by Terry Wild Stock

My sister Katelyn loves dogs, and they adore her right back. When we tried taking Katelyn's picture, our dog Daisy kept interrupting.

Amy Swartzentruber
Denmark, South Carolina

Imagine my surprise when I caught this squirrel enjoying every last bit of the birdseed!

Lynne Berghoff
Howell, New Jersey

▲ This eastern bluebird puffs up against the cold on a 15-degree day at Merrill Creek Reservoir in New Jersey.

Charlie Trapani
Easton, Pennsylvania

▲ Our granddaughter Hannah says goodbye to Vink after her seventh birthday party.

Alice Simmons
Front Royal, Virginia

▶ My daughters, Madelyn and Autumn, hide inside the 1,674-pound pumpkin that I grew.

Kevin Marsh
Parker, South Dakota

▼ I take a different route home every beautiful fall day so I can enjoy the colors of the trees and of the crops in farm fields like this one.

Charlotte Pletcher
Somerset, Pennsylvania

The Green River Covered Bridge
invites travelers to take a trip back
in time to 1800s New England.
Photo by Paul Rezendes

"Autumn carries more gold in its pocket than all the other seasons."

Jim Bishop

▲ Toby the pony is lucky to have such a fine friend as Ryann. As you can see, Ryann's already quite the young horsewoman, confidently holding Toby's rope and assuring him with a comforting pet on the neck.
Becky Charvat
Mandan, North Dakota

▶ One day I looked out my window to see tom turkeys strutting their stuff. When viewing my pictures later, I noticed their heads had formed a heart!

Kristine Cooley
Wayzata, Minnesota

▲ I spotted this barn surrounded by vibrant fall foliage while traveling through northern West Virginia.

John Brueske
St. Charles, Minnesota

▲ These two Canada geese looked as though they were walking on water when they chased each other on Stagecoach Lake.

Bradley Moser
Hickman, Nebraska

At 1,200 feet, Crabtree Falls in Virginia is one of the highest cascading waterfalls east of the Mississippi River.
Photo by Pat & Chuck Blackley

▲ I had to move away to the big city and come back to my hometown before I could truly appreciate the beauty of the country, especially in the fall.

Mike Contos
Naples, NY

The setting sun casts a glow over Sam's Throne Recreation Area in the Ozarks of Arkansas.
Photo by Paul Caldwell

**At dusk, the sun gives way to the moon in Joshua Tree National Park.
Photo by Laurence Parent**

▲ While savoring the last of the crab apples, this blue jay didn't seem to mind me taking his picture.

Rachel Fark
New Bremen, Ohio

◄ My friend's little girl Beth found the perfect pumpkin at Schilter Family Farm in Washington's Nisqually Valley, and she was pretty sure she could carry it home all by herself.

Naomi Williams
Olympia, Washington

Heart & Soul

FEEL THE LOVE OF COUNTRY

Friend John McCarther hitches a ride north of Nebraska's Ash Hollow State Historical Park.

Every morning we thank the Lord for His blessings and ask Him to have someone step forward to help us find a place to camp that night.

Ken and David began the trip in St. Francis, Kansas (right) and shared meals along the way.

Hitch Up the Haflingers

Trinity Lutheran Church stands on the Great Western Cattle Trail south of Ogallala, Nebraska.

My daughters called it "man-o-pause." When I turned 50, I told my wife, Linda, I wasn't getting any younger and was thinking about buying that motorcycle every man dreams of. Well, as all good women do, she decided that sounded dangerous and pointed me in another direction—back toward horses.

I'm a farmer, and I grew up riding and driving horses with my dad. Our family had always raised quarter horses. But, after the kids grew out of 4-H and Little Britches Rodeo, and my old driving team horses and roping horse passed away, I didn't replace them. Then one day an Amish friend, Glenn Yetzey, told me, "You should try purebred Haflingers. You won't be disappointed."

So in 2004, I purchased a team of Haflinger geldings. They were full brothers: 2-year-old Barney and 3-year-old Buster. Then I came up with all kinds of ways to incorporate my "boys" into our life, from planting potatoes, haying, road grading and mowing to church hayrides, parades and Sunday afternoon trail rides. I am always amazed at their calmness and willingness to please.

Then, one evening when I was talking on the phone to my old high school buddy Ken Kleinsorge about the Great Western Cattle Trail, I said, "Wouldn't it be fun to experience what it was like?"

Ken, a finish carpenter who owns a remodeling business over in Greeley, Colorado, replied, "You know, we're not getting any younger." And suddenly we were planning a chuck wagon trip.

It took two years to get everything together. I pulled my 1883 lumber wagon out of the shed, and Ken helped build the chuck wagon cook box, complete with a water barrel, toolbox, and the all-important coffee grinder. We talked to experts and judges of chuck wagon cook-offs to make sure the experience would be as authentic as possible. Sewing the tarps took several long days with the help of my wife, who was now wondering about the wisdom of starting this whole thing.

In September of 2011, Ken and I finally headed north from St. Francis, Kansas, to experience what it would have been like to drive the chuck wagon on an old-time cattle drive. I drove the wagon while Ken rode his mule, Babe. We stayed off the main highways, took country roads and aimed to travel about 100 miles at 15 miles a day. That first year, we made it up to Champion, Nebraska.

In 2012, I added two more Haflingers (Bill and Bob) to the team to give us twice as much horsepower in the hills. We started where we left off in Champion and headed north. But we woke up one morning to about 6 inches of snow and 18 degrees. I've worked outdoors all my life, but I don't think I've ever been so cold.

We pushed on for two more days, and finally Ken said, "For two cents, I'd quit this right now."

And I said, "Well, I've got two cents, and I wish you'd told me that two days ago!" So we only made it up to Grant that year. The next year we went from Ogallala to Oshkosh. Last year we made it to Bridgeport in the western panhandle. This year, we're planning to cross the border into Wyoming near Torrington.

We usually put in 12-hour days. It takes about three hours to break camp in the morning. Then we spend six hours on the trail. Then it takes about three hours to set up camp and cook dinner. Like Ken says, "By the time you make breakfast, pull down the camp, pull the wagon, then stop and set it all back up again, you're wore out."

Each evening we stretch out a canvas attached to the back of the chuck wagon to provide shelter. The wagon's tailgate drops down to form a table where we prepare dinner. We do all of our cooking in cast-iron Dutch ovens, and we end every meal with an extra-big cobbler that we share with the 15-20 people who usually come around to see what we're up to.

Everywhere we go, people talk to us. They tell stories about the area and give advice on the best routes. Every morning we thank the Lord for His blessings and ask Him to have someone step forward to help us find a place to camp that night. And every day on every trip for four years, somebody has. It's been quite an experience.

The trips also got us into cooking chuck wagon meals for benefits. We're feeding 500 people this week, and we cooked for 200 last week. You hear a lot about cowboy stew, but our biggest crowd-pleaser is always chicken fried steak, mashed potatoes and gravy, peach cobbler and, if we're lucky, homemade ice cream.

Cooking for that many people isn't easy, and most days on the trail are even harder work. But we have a lot of fun. My wife was right; I didn't need that motorcycle after all.

David Pabst
Colby, Kansas

A Treasured Teacher

Visiting my grandma Lillian Klassy Hefty always makes my week. She turned 100 recently, and for 39 of those years I've benefited from her love and support. But Grandma also earns my respect as a person. When not farming and raising children, she taught school with an uncommon enthusiasm that made her a local legend.

In 1933, armed with her County Normal certificate and a yellow notebook for recording students' progress, Miss Klassy started teaching at Marty School, a one-room rural schoolhouse. When she married, the old-fashioned rules required her to leave her post. But she stayed involved in education, becoming her district's first female school board president.

After her children were grown, Grandma returned to teaching. When district rules required her to upgrade her teaching certificate, she graduated magna cum laude from the University of Wisconsin.

During my growing-up years, we made weekly trips to town together for errands. Everyone seemed to be either a former student or the parent of one, and all shared praise and warm memories. Through these trips, I discovered who my grandmother was in the eyes of the community. One day we were at the deli, where Grandma ordered a half-pound of baby Swiss. The clerk leaned over the glass and said, "Lillian, my daughter still talks about your class. I think she became a teacher because she loved you so much."

I can't count the people I've seen approach Grandma over the years, but each person added to my picture of the kind of woman she is. If a student didn't have lunch, Grandma sneaked hers into the child's book bag. When she saw that students were afraid to try a new vegetable in the cafeteria line, she'd get a double helping and encourage them to take a nibble. I learned this in the produce aisle one day, when a woman buying beets smiled at us and told Grandma, "I still like these because of you." I even met the former student who engraved "Mrs. Hefty" on a wooden sign for her classroom—a sign that still hangs in her apartment to this day.

One student in particular was grateful for Grandma's encouragement. He stood straight and proud as he told her how he'd completed high school, then college. Later, she explained that as a boy, he'd planned to drop out, as his parents and siblings had. But Grandma told him he was the brightest student in class and he could do anything. I imagine him as a boy, nervously confiding in Grandma, and her saying what she always said to her students, kids and grandkids: "Just do your best."

Today I look around her home and see mementos that prove she took her own advice. It's filled with gifts from pupils, including a quilt sewn and presented to her by one of her first classes. And she still keeps a handwritten notebook of all her students' names going back to her first class in 1933.

Yet there's something you won't see in her home, a lesson Grandma has no idea she taught me. Just by being someone people regularly thanked, she showed me how gratitude affects the recipient. I'd notice the way she'd come alive, and I know that these encounters contributed to her many vibrant years.

I'm not a teacher, but I try to honor Grandma by going out of my way to thank educators who don't work in small communities where people greet them like family. If Grandma taught me anything, it's that doing my best in all the tiny everyday moments will add up over a lifetime to make a beautiful difference in the world.

Anne Veit
Middleton, Wisconsin

Marty School, circa 1900

Lillian holds her first teaching certificate, dated 1933.

Grandma and granddaughter smile for a selfie. Anne (right) snaps these fun shots every chance she gets.

When a dirt road lies ahead, you know you're in the country.

An Ode to the Road

Dirt roads are the best. Not gravel. Not pavement. Maybe this is because dirt roads are, as Robert Frost put it, less traveled. Perhaps it's because they lead to some great farm ponds. Or maybe it's because a dirt road was the only way to get to our home near Stillwater, Oklahoma.

Although people have spread tons of gravel on that road over the years, it insists on clinging to its dirt heritage. With the first soaking rain, it swallows every trace of gravel. This road can go from surface dust to knee-deep, greasy ruts rivaling the most challenging off-road excursion, then back to dust in 24 hours.

It's an exercise in futility when road graders try scraping gravel from the ditches back onto the dirt road. The result is a substratum of nails, broken bottles and other random hazards that has given me lots of practice at patching tires.

Not every intersection on a dirt road has a stop sign, and johnsongrass as high as a bison's eye may obscure your vision. Loose gravel on my road helped prepare me for driving on the ice in Pennsylvania, where my family and I now live.

Besides getting me ready for a position on an Indy 500 pit crew, a dirt road has many other benefits. It's a great place to see wildlife: roadrunners, deer, coyotes, rabbits, turkeys, bobwhite and more. And there's always hope for a Sasquatch sighting.

Plus, the dust cloud I stir up as I barrel down a dirt road lets the kids and me pretend we're deploying a clever smoke screen to outwit an imaginary pursuer.

And although these roads are a good place to see the sights or take a teenager to practice driving, rural folks live along them and have places they need to be. So if you're a dirt-road newcomer, do not wander around taking up both lanes.

If you do meet another vehicle, probably a pickup, do not forget to acknowledge the driver. This is a critical component of back-road etiquette. While this communication can take place on any two-lane road, it's more intimate on dirt roads. Properly executed, it turns complete strangers into friends for life.

I don't mean a full arm-flopping wave or salute; this is a subtle, casual exchange. It could be a simple nod or a quick tip of the chin, but often it's just the carefully timed lifting of one finger off the steering wheel.

They recently tried to pave my dirt road, and now, when I go home, I catch myself looking longingly down some of the side dirt roads on my way into Stillwater. But I know that my friendly old dirt road waits patiently beneath.

Andy Whitcomb
St. Petersburg, Pennsylvania

Uncle Leland (riding his favorite horse, Cricket) was the real deal.

One 'Yee-Haw' Too Many

My heroes have always been cowboys. The words of that old Willie Nelson song ring very true for me. Early on I favored Roy Rogers, Gene Autry and Hopalong Cassidy. Then I moved on to John Wayne and Clint Eastwood as my tastes matured and grew more refined.

But I finally figured out that all my heroes were just playing the part, except for one. My uncle Leland Hallmark was the genuine article, from the soles of his worn boots to the top of his hat—which he put on his head whenever he left the house.

My earliest memories of Uncle Leland come from visiting him and his family on a ranch south of Llano, Texas, in Hill Country. It was a beautiful place for a kid whose main passion, other than baseball, was to ride horses all over the prairie.

I was full-grown when I found out Leland didn't own the ranch; he was the ranch foreman. But it didn't matter to me. He made his living on the back of a horse just like all my other heroes. My little brother, Glenn, was equally crazy about cowboys, and we thought Uncle Leland must have hung the moon while sitting on top of his favorite horse, Cricket.

My only problem with Leland was his cowboy hat. It was always bent in strange directions. It was dirty. And worst of all, it wasn't white. Whenever we visited I made it a point to fix his hat for him. I preferred the Roy Rogers look, so I worked real hard on his hat every night. And every evening when he came home from work, the hat would be a mess again.

One day Leland left before sunrise—with a freshly arranged hat—to gather all the cows that needed treatment from the local veterinarian.

He was gone all day. Toward sunset, Glenn and I were sitting on the porch, sipping cool water from the well, when we saw Leland slowly working a small herd of cows toward a corral next to the barn. We got so excited we nearly fell over each other running to the rail fence to welcome him home, yelling at the top of our lungs, "YEE-HAW! RIDE 'EM, COWBOY!"

The look on Leland's face was slightly less surprised than the look on the faces of all those cows. I've never seen that many cows run in that many directions in all my life. It was so exciting, Glenn wet his pants. Granted, it didn't take too much for Glenn to wet his pants back then, but let me tell you, it was really exciting.

Our momma came running with a look on her face that scared us silly. We didn't know why she was mad at us, but we ran and hid anyway. She finally found us in the barn. Leland didn't make it back home again with the cows for another four hours, so she had plenty of time to explain why she was upset with us.

Leland, on the other hand, didn't seem too mad at all. He handed me his hat, ate a quick bite of supper and then went to bed. Because that's what heroes do.

Russell Mihills
Hurst, Texas

Please, Don't Want This Puppy!

It was the first week of November. I was 13 years old, standing outside the automatic sliding doors of our local discount store. Mom sat in front of me in a lawn chair, holding a pup, while my sister was at her feet, busy with the box holding the rest of the puppies—except for mine.

I stood with my back to the parking lot, sheltered from the wind by a concrete column. It was cold, but my denim jacket kept me fairly warm. I hoped it was doing the same for the little ball of golden fur in my arms. I glanced down and got a lick on my chin. Her name was Libby.

I stood as far back from the doors as possible. Maybe nobody would see me. Maybe it would be 5 p.m. soon, and we could go home. Those brown eyes seemed to be pleading with me, and I wanted to run back to the van with her.

I'd never had a dog of my very own, much less one as adorable as this puppy, with her big brown eyes and snip of white on her forehead. She was gold and soft as silk, and she'd captured my heart the moment I saw her. But reality was harsh. We already had two dogs. We just couldn't keep this pup.

Still, maybe nobody would notice her snuggled down inside my jacket. I desperately clung to that hope as the minutes stretched into an hour and longer. My hat wasn't keeping my ears warm, and I worried that Libby couldn't stand the cold much longer either.

Then Mom said, "Hey, Meg, go see if that lady wants a puppy." I looked across the parking lot and saw a woman waving at us from a parked truck. I ran over.

"Are they free?" she asked.

"Yes. They're 6 weeks old."

"I'll take this one," she replied, and held out her arms. I didn't have time to think about it. I just handed my puppy to a complete stranger.

"Her name is Libby," I said. The lady nodded—a very cool and uninterested nod—then turned her attention to the pup on her lap and rolled up the window.

I walked slowly back to the store and hid from the wind behind the concrete pillar. That was it. Libby was gone. I was never going to see my sweet girl again.

A few minutes later, a little girl of about 8 or 9 came out of the store and walked across the parking lot to the truck. She opened the door and climbed inside.

As the woman drove away, I caught a glimpse of the girl laughing as a squirming, tail-wagging puppy left canine kisses all over her face.

Libby was already making another little girl happy. I pulled my hat down over my ears and managed a little smile on that cold, windy November day.

Megan Cook
Bear Lake, Michigan

Megan loved Libby from the first day.

I'd never had a dog of my very own...
she was gold and soft as silk, and she'd
captured my heart the moment I saw her.

Best-Laid Plans

The year might have been 1970 or earlier, when my brother, Greg, and his wife, Linda, invited us to their new home for Thanksgiving. My husband, our two little girls and I lived on our small farm in the Catskill Mountains with a few horses, goats, chickens and dogs. My brother's house was at least three and a half hours south, but it would be such fun to see the family. I sure did miss them.

That week I baked bread and my famous apple pies and made a bucketload of coleslaw. I added several jars of my homemade green tomato pickles to the menu, and my husband picked up some delicious local apple cider.

My good friend Martha, who lived a few miles up the road, promised to feed our horses if we didn't get home in time for the late feeding. Her folks and sisters were driving up from the city for Thanksgiving, so she bought the biggest turkey she could find. While Martha cleaned her house and got ready for her company, I peeled apples, kneaded dough and shredded cabbage for coleslaw.

Everything was ready for our early-morning departure. I fell asleep thinking of the fun we would have.

I bounced out of bed at the first sound of the alarm. When I put the coffeepot on, I noticed movement outside the window above the sink. I turned on the outside light and saw snowflakes. The unexpected flurry was about 15 inches deep and still falling.

There would be no trip. The car couldn't get out of the driveway. I let the family sleep peacefully and tried to get over my disappointment—no relatives and no turkey.

I quietly put on my coat and boots and trudged through that stupid snow to take care of the animals.

The girls were in their rooms pouting when our party line rang a few minutes before 9 a.m.

"Bummer, huh?" Martha said.

"It is!" I replied. "At least we have lots of apple pies, bread and coleslaw. Are your folks going to try to come up from the city?"

"Oh, no!" she said. "It's even worse in the city. Maddie was supposed to bring dessert and salad. We don't have much else! Just the turkey!"

"Hey!" we both said at once.

I packed the coleslaw, pickles, bread, cider and apple pies. We secured the food on our toboggan and spent almost two hours breaking a trail through the fluffy new snow.

No one complained about the long walk or cold, wet feet. We got to Martha's just in time. That day, we talked about the things we were thankful for: health, happiness, wonderful friends, warm homes, good neighbors and enough food for an army.

The return trip in the sparkling, snowy twilight was so peaceful. I've enjoyed many Thanksgivings since, but the memory of that snowy one is the clearest of all. It taught me that God could turn disappointments into surprise blessings. I am so thankful I learned that lesson.

Joyce Carroll
Accord, New York

> We talked about the things we were thankful for: health, happiness, wonderful friends, warm homes, good neighbors and enough food for an army.

Joyce and her family broke a trail through fluffy snow on foot one Thanksgiving.

Nancy took 1-week-old Garrett hiking in Glacier National Park (above). At left, Garrett, nearly 3, examines the logs of an old homestead.

Raising Little Explorers

I made a New Year's resolution when I became a mom to spend at least 15 minutes outdoors every day, finding inspiration in nature. Doing so renews my mind and sets me on a positive track so I can tackle the tasks that come with raising children, managing a household and working. Even when I feel like I don't have the time, I engage in this simple, uplifting activity. I know those few minutes outside will pay dividends later when I return recharged.

It hasn't always been easy to get away, but I know I am forming lifelong habits that Garrett, my almost-3-year-old son, and Dylan, my 9-month-old daughter, will enjoy with me.

We often sneak away to see what we can find. Now our hikes are completed at a toddler's pace and distance, and I never cease to be amazed by all the adventures we uncover in every season.

One warm spring afternoon, we set out to explore the mud puddles along our lane. For over an hour, we threw pinecones and sticks into the larger ones and, of course, splashed around in the smaller ones, soaking ourselves in the process.

While I was busy digging up transplants for a new garden bed one summer morning, Garrett came over to me, frantic that a snake was on the mat where he and his sister were busy playing with trucks. I asked him to show me, and he pointed at a caterpillar.

Transplants abandoned, we caught the caterpillar and had an impromptu biology lesson about how caterpillars eat leaves, form little chrysalises and

then emerge as butterflies. That began a caterpillar craze that lasted for weeks.

Fall is my favorite time of year, and I usually steer our adventures to include listening for elk bugling. After one hike at a nearby trailhead, we weren't sure that Garrett had heard the high-pitched squeal and guttural whomps from a distant bull elk. On the ride home, his dad and I were discussing how we never tire of that sound. Then we heard an impressive imitation of a bull elk bugle coming from our toddler in the back seat. Since that day, we occasionally hear the wild sound of an elk calling from our living room.

When extreme cold keeps Garrett, Dylan and me indoors, we enjoy nature from our window. We place bird feeders and suet cakes within easy viewing distance and spend time identifying, counting and recording the species that frequent our feeders. We especially love spotting species that come along by chance: rabbits, mice, squirrels, deer, flying squirrels and raptors.

And if you think the time for exploring the outdoors has passed beneath a blanket of snow, think again. The best time to explore nature is in winter. Tracking in the snow opens up a whole world of seeing.

Sharing these experiences with children can open your eyes to things that you would otherwise take for granted. May the New Year bring you and your children opportunities to answer the call of the wild!

Nancy Schwalm
Lincoln, Montana

Mud Pie Magic

Despite all his hard work, Daddy always made time for a memorable moment.

Every last crumb of that mud pie seems to go in Daddy's mouth as little Linda watches with a mix of pride and surprise.

My daddy was a small-scale farmer and rancher. Despite his hard work and his farming know-how, his profits were low. This meant that we didn't have what most folks would call nice things. However, I was having too much fun as a kid to know that I was poor.

I spent many a day cooking outdoors. In the mornings, my portable kitchen would be on the back porch, where the concrete slab made a nice kitchen floor. When the noon sun appeared, I loaded my pots and pans into my little red wagon and hauled my kitchen to the front porch.

It was amazing what goodies I could prepare with such basic ingredients as dirt, water, grass, rocks and flowers. I could whip up anything from fried chicken to chocolate cake.

I never tired of my kitchen chores. No, I didn't have

a microwave to speed up the meal preparation or an automatic dishwasher to do the dishes. I knew Mom and Dad would love me even with dishpan hands.

My "kids" loved me, too. I had six little charges in all: four cats, one dog and one rabbit. They were good kids, always well-behaved and never complaining.

Of course, I didn't spend all my waking hours in my play kitchen. There was also real work around the farm, and one of my favorite early chores was bottle-feeding three motherless Jersey calves. Daddy had bought them thinking one of our cows would adopt them, but our cow had different thoughts. That was OK. I had fun feeding them and naming them: Peanuts, Popcorn and Cracker Jacks.

And life on the farm could be dangerous. I found myself on many occasions fighting wild, bloodthirsty rustlers in the peach

orchard. With my stick horse and six-shooter, I always saved the day.

But all my heroic moments couldn't compare to my special moments with Daddy. I remember one chilly day when I was 5 years old like it was yesterday. I met my dad coming around the house. He was wearing his big, heavy Army coat he got while he was in the Korean War. He asked me if I would fix him something to eat.

I began preparing one of my famous mud pies and handed him a plate. Daddy placed each bite right up to his mouth, and I believed he'd eaten it all, because he returned a clean plate. I was so astonished that I raced into the house to tell Mom.

My daddy had a way of always making me feel very special. Even something as simple as a plate full of mud pies became magical.

Linda McDaniel
Huntsville, Texas

A Taste of Autumn

SAVOR THE FLAVORS OF THE SEASON

Asparagus, Bacon & Herbed Cheese Pizza

START TO FINISH: 30 MIN. • **MAKES:** 6 SERVINGS

INGREDIENTS

- 1   prebaked 12-inch pizza crust
- 6   teaspoons olive oil, divided
- 1   cup shredded part-skim mozzarella cheese
- 2¼ cups cut fresh asparagus (1-inch pieces)
- 8   bacon strips, cooked and crumbled
- ½   cup garlic-herb spreadable cheese (about 3 ounces)
- ¼   teaspoon crushed red pepper flakes

DIRECTIONS

1. Preheat oven to 450°. Place crust on an ungreased 12-in. pizza pan or baking sheet; brush the top with 4 teaspoons oil. Top with mozzarella cheese, asparagus and bacon. Drop spreadable cheese by teaspoonfuls over pizza. Sprinkle with pepper flakes; drizzle with remaining oil.
2. Bake 12-15 minutes or until cheese is lightly browned.

Campfire Peach Cobbler

PREP: 25 MIN. • **COOK:** 30 MIN. + STANDING
MAKES: 8 SERVINGS

INGREDIENTS

- 2 cups all-purpose flour
- 1 cup sugar
- 4 teaspoons baking powder
- ½ teaspoon salt
- 1 cup 2% milk
- ½ cup butter, melted

FILLING

- 2 cans (15¼ ounces each) sliced peaches
- ¼ cup sugar
- ½ teaspoon ground cinnamon, optional

DIRECTIONS

1. Prepare the campfire or grill for low heat, using 32-40 charcoal briquettes.
2. Line the inside of a 10-in. Dutch oven with heavy-duty foil. In a large bowl, whisk together the first four ingredients. Add milk and melted butter, stirring just until moistened. Pour into prepared pan.
3. Drain peaches, reserving 1 cup syrup. Arrange peaches over batter; sprinkle with sugar and, if desired, cinnamon. Pour reserved syrup over fruit. Place lid on Dutch oven.
4. When briquettes are covered with white ash, place Dutch oven directly on half of the briquettes. Using long-handled tongs, place remaining briquettes on top of pan lid. Cook for 30-40 minutes or until cobbler is set and beginning to brown, using tongs to lift lid carefully when checking. If necessary, cook 5 minutes longer. Remove from heat; let stand, uncovered, 15 minutes before serving.

Pull-Apart Caramel Coffee Cake

PREP: 10 MIN. • **BAKE:** 25 MIN.
MAKES: 1 LOAF (16 SERVINGS)

INGREDIENTS

- 2 tubes (12 ounces each) refrigerated buttermilk biscuits
- 1 cup packed brown sugar
- ½ cup heavy whipping cream
- 1 teaspoon ground cinnamon

DIRECTIONS

1. Preheat oven to 350°. Cut each biscuit into four pieces; arrange evenly in a 10-in. fluted tube pan coated with cooking spray. In a small bowl, mix remaining ingredients until blended; pour over biscuits.
2. Bake 25-30 minutes or until golden brown. Cool in pan for 5 minutes before inverting onto a serving plate.

Maple Ricotta Mousse with Candied Pecans

PREP: 25 MIN. + COOLING
MAKES: 4 SERVINGS

INGREDIENTS

- ⅔ cup maple syrup
- ¼ cup chopped pecans
- ½ cup heavy whipping cream
- 1¼ cups whole-milk ricotta cheese
- ½ cup mascarpone cheese

DIRECTIONS

1. Place syrup in a small saucepan; bring to a boil. Reduce heat; simmer, uncovered, 5 minutes. Transfer to a bowl; cool completely.

2. In a small heavy skillet, cook and stir pecans over medium heat, about 3 minutes. Drizzle with 1 tablespoon cooked syrup; cook and stir 1 minute longer. Spread on foil to cool.

3. In a small bowl, beat cream until soft peaks form. In a large bowl, beat ricotta and mascarpone cheeses until light and fluffy. Gradually beat in ⅓ cup cooled syrup; gently fold in whipped cream.

4. To serve, spoon mousse into dessert dishes. Drizzle with remaining cooled syrup; top with candied pecans.

Balsamic Roasted Chicken Thighs with Root Vegetables

PREP: 15 MIN. + MARINATING • **BAKE:** 35 MIN. • **MAKES:** 6 SERVINGS

INGREDIENTS

- 4 tablespoons olive oil, divided
- 3 tablespoons stone-ground mustard
- 2 tablespoons balsamic vinaigrette
- ¾ teaspoon kosher salt, divided
- ¾ teaspoon freshly ground pepper, divided
- 6 bone-in chicken thighs (about 2¼ pounds)
- 4 medium parsnips, peeled and cut into ½-inch pieces
- 1 medium sweet potato, peeled and cut into ½-inch pieces
- 4 shallots, chopped
- ¼ teaspoon caraway seeds
- 4 tablespoons minced fresh parsley, divided
- 3 bacon strips, cooked and crumbled, divided

DIRECTIONS

1. In a bowl, whisk 3 tablespoons oil, mustard, balsamic vinaigrette and ½ teaspoon each salt and pepper until blended. Add chicken, turning to coat. Refrigerate, covered, 6 hours or overnight.

2. Preheat oven to 425°. Place chicken, skin side up, on half of a greased 15x10x1-in. baking pan. Place parsnips and sweet potato in a large bowl; add shallots, caraway seeds and the remaining oil, salt and pepper and toss to combine. Arrange in a single layer on remaining half of pan.

3. Roast chicken and vegetables for 20 minutes. Stir vegetables; roast chicken and vegetables 15-20 minutes longer or until a thermometer inserted in chicken reads 170°-175° and vegetables are tender.

4. Transfer vegetables to a bowl; toss with 2 tablespoons parsley and half of the bacon. Serve chicken with vegetables; sprinkle chicken with the remaining parsley and bacon.

Empanada Beef Chili

PREP: 20 MIN. • **COOK:** 1½ HOURS • **MAKES:** 6 SERVINGS

INGREDIENTS

1½ pounds boneless beef chuck steak, cut into ¾-inch pieces
½ teaspoon salt
½ teaspoon pepper
4 teaspoons canola oil, divided
1 medium onion, chopped
2 garlic cloves, minced
1 can (6 ounces) tomato paste
2 teaspoons ground chipotle pepper
2 teaspoons ground cinnamon
2½ cups beef broth
1 can (4 ounces) chopped green chilies
½ cup raisins
3 tablespoons minced fresh cilantro
1 can (15 ounces) black beans, rinsed and drained
1 can (2¼ ounces) sliced ripe olives, drained
    Optional toppings: shredded Mexican cheese blend, minced fresh cilantro and chopped walnuts

DIRECTIONS

1. Toss beef with salt and pepper. In a Dutch oven, heat 2 teaspoons oil over medium heat. Brown beef in batches; remove from pan.
2. Add onion and the remaining oil to same pan; cook and stir for 2-3 minutes or until onion is tender. Add garlic; cook 1 minute longer. Stir in tomato paste, chipotle pepper and cinnamon; cook and stir 3 minutes. Stir in broth, green chilies, raisins and cilantro. Return beef to pan; bring to a boil. Reduce heat; simmer, covered, 1 hour or until beef is tender.
3. Stir in beans and olives; cook, uncovered, 10 minutes. If desired, serve with toppings.

Maple Glazed Squash

PREP: 15 MIN. • **BAKE:** 50 MIN. • **MAKES:** 6 SERVINGS

INGREDIENTS

2 medium acorn squash
¼ teaspoon salt
⅛ teaspoon pepper
1 cup maple syrup
1 medium tart apple, peeled and chopped
2 tablespoons raisins, optional
1 teaspoon ground cinnamon

DIRECTIONS

1. Preheat oven to 350°. Cut squash lengthwise in half; remove and discard seeds. Cut halves crosswise into 1-in. slices; discard ends. Place squash in a greased 13x9-in. baking dish; sprinkle with salt and pepper.
2. In a small bowl, mix remaining ingredients; pour over squash. Bake, covered, 50-60 minutes or until squash is tender.

Gingersnap Crumb Pear Pie

PREP: 35 MIN. + CHILLING • **BAKE:** 1 HOUR + COOLING • **MAKES:** 8 SERVINGS

INGREDIENTS

Pastry for single-crust pie
(9 inches)

TOPPING
- 1 cup crushed gingersnap cookies
  (about 16 cookies)
- ¼ cup all-purpose flour
- ¼ cup packed brown sugar
- Pinch salt
- ½ cup cold butter, cubed

FILLING
- ⅔ cup sugar
- ⅓ cup all-purpose flour
- ½ teaspoon ground ginger
- ¼ teaspoon salt
- 2½ pounds ripe pears
  (about 4 medium), peeled
  and thinly sliced
- 1 tablespoon lemon juice
- 1 teaspoon vanilla extract
- Hot caramel ice cream
  topping, optional

DIRECTIONS

1. On a lightly floured surface, roll pastry dough to a ⅛-in.-thick circle; transfer to a 9-in. pie plate. Trim and flute edge. Refrigerate for 30 minutes. Preheat oven to 400°.

2. Line unpricked pastry dough with a double thickness of foil. Fill with pie weights, dried beans or uncooked rice. Bake for 15-20 minutes or until the edges are light golden brown. Remove foil and weights; bake for 3-6 minutes longer or until bottom is golden brown. Cool on a wire rack. Reduce oven setting to 350°.

3. For topping, in a food processor, combine crushed cookies, flour, brown sugar and salt. Add butter; pulse until crumbly.

4. For filling, in a large bowl, mix sugar, flour, ginger and salt. Add pears, lemon juice and vanilla; toss gently to combine. Transfer to crust; cover with topping.

5. Place pie on a baking sheet; bake for 60-70 minutes or until topping is lightly browned and pears are tender. Cover loosely with foil during the last 15 minutes if necessary to prevent overbrowning. Cool on a wire rack at least 1 hour before serving. If desired, drizzle with caramel topping.

PASTRY FOR 9-INCH SINGLE-CRUST PIE
Combine 1¼ cups all-purpose flour and ¼ teaspoon salt; cut in ½ cup cold butter until crumbly. Gradually add 3-5 tablespoons ice water, tossing with a fork until the dough holds together when pressed. Wrap dough in plastic and refrigerate 1 hour.

NOTE Let pie weights cool before storing. Beans and rice may be used again for pie weights, but not for cooking.

Pull-Apart Bacon Bread
PREP: 20 MIN. + RISING • **BAKE:** 55 MIN.
MAKES: 1 LOAF (16 SERVINGS)

INGREDIENTS
- 12 bacon strips, diced
- 1 loaf (1 pound) frozen bread dough, thawed
- 2 tablespoons olive oil, divided
- 1 cup shredded part-skim mozzarella cheese
- 1 envelope (1 ounce) ranch salad dressing mix

DIRECTIONS
1. In a large skillet, cook bacon over medium heat for 5 minutes or until partially cooked; drain on paper towels. Roll out dough to ½-in. thickness; brush with 1 tablespoon of oil. Cut into 1-in. pieces; place in a large bowl. Add the bacon, mozzarella, dressing mix and remaining oil; toss to coat.
2. Arrange pieces in a 9x5-in. oval on a parchment paper-lined baking sheet, layering as needed. Cover and let rise in a warm place for 30 minutes or until doubled.
3. Bake at 350° for 40 minutes. Cover with foil; bake 15 minutes longer or until golden brown.

Shoepeg Corn Side Dish
PREP: 20 MIN. • **COOK:** 3 HOURS
MAKES: 8 SERVINGS

INGREDIENTS
- 1 can (14½ ounces) French-style green beans, drained
- 2 cans (7 ounces each) white or shoepeg corn
- 1 can (10¾ ounces) condensed cream of mushroom soup, undiluted
- 1 jar (4½ ounces) sliced mushrooms, drained
- ½ cup slivered almonds
- ½ cup shredded cheddar cheese
- ½ cup sour cream
- ¾ cup French-fried onions

DIRECTIONS
In a 3-qt. slow cooker, combine the first seven ingredients. Cover and cook on low for 3-4 hours or until vegetables are tender, stirring occasionally. Sprinkle with onions during the last 15 minutes of cooking.

Sausage Bread Dressing

PREP: 30 MIN. • **BAKE:** 40 MIN. • **MAKES:** ABOUT 12 CUPS

INGREDIENTS

- 4 cups seasoned stuffing cubes
- 1 cup cornbread stuffing mix (about 3 ounces)
- ½ pound bulk Italian sausage
- 1 large onion, chopped
- 3 tablespoons butter
- 1 large tart apple, peeled and chopped
- 1⅓ cups sliced fresh shiitake mushrooms (about 4 ounces)
- 1¼ cups sliced fresh mushrooms (about 4 ounces)
- 1 celery rib, chopped
- ½ cup minced fresh parsley
- 1 tablespoon fresh sage or 1 teaspoon dried sage leaves
- ⅛ teaspoon salt
- ⅛ teaspoon pepper
- 1 can (14½ ounces) chicken broth
- 1 cup pecan halves

DIRECTIONS

1. Preheat oven to 325°. In a large bowl, combine stuffing cubes and stuffing mix.
2. In a large skillet, cook sausage and onion over medium heat 4-6 minutes or until meat is no longer pink, breaking up sausage into crumbles. Remove from pan with a slotted spoon and add to stuffing mixture.
3. Add butter to the same pan. Add apple, mushrooms and celery; cook and stir over medium-high heat until the mushrooms are tender. Stir in parsley, sage, salt and pepper. Stir into stuffing mixture. Stir in broth and pecans.
4. Transfer to a greased 3-qt. baking dish. Bake, covered, for 30 minutes. Uncover; bake 10 minutes longer or until lightly browned.

Campfire Cinnamon Twists

START TO FINISH: 25 MIN.
MAKES: 16 SERVINGS

INGREDIENTS

- ¼ cup sugar
- 2 teaspoons ground cinnamon
- 1 tube (12.4 ounces) refrigerated cinnamon rolls with icing
- 2 tablespoons butter, melted

DIRECTIONS

1. Mix sugar and cinnamon. Remove icing from cinnamon rolls; transfer to a resealable plastic bag for drizzling.
2. Separate rolls; cut each in half. Roll the halves into 6-in. ropes. Wrap each rope tightly around a long metal skewer, beginning ½ in. from pointed end; pinch each end to secure.
3. Cook rolls over a hot campfire until golden brown, about 5 minutes, turning occasionally. Brush with butter; sprinkle with sugar mixture. Cut a small hole in one corner of icing bag. Drizzle icing over twists.

Handcrafted with Love

CREATE A FEELING OF HOME

Zigzag Fab

Glam up a pumpkin with some tape and a can of spray paint.

WHAT YOU'LL NEED

Pumpkins
Painter's tape
Interior spray paint

DIRECTIONS

1. For chevron stripes, mark off the desired depth of the chevron (ours is 2½ in.) on 1-in.-wide painter's tape. Cut several lengths. Mark the widest point around the pumpkin's circumference with a pencil. Position a length of tape on a 30- to 45-degree angle so that the bottom corner touches the center guideline. Apply lengths of tape around the pumpkin at the same angle, with one corner of each piece touching the center mark. Overlap the pieces at the ends to form a continuous line. Add stripes above and below the center about 1 in. apart to complete design. Tape over stem.
2. Working quickly in a well-ventilated area, spray-paint pumpkin. Wait a minute or two. Spray on a second coat.
3. Wait a minute or so and then remove tape strips. Do this while the paint is still tacky to prevent chipping. Let paint dry thoroughly.

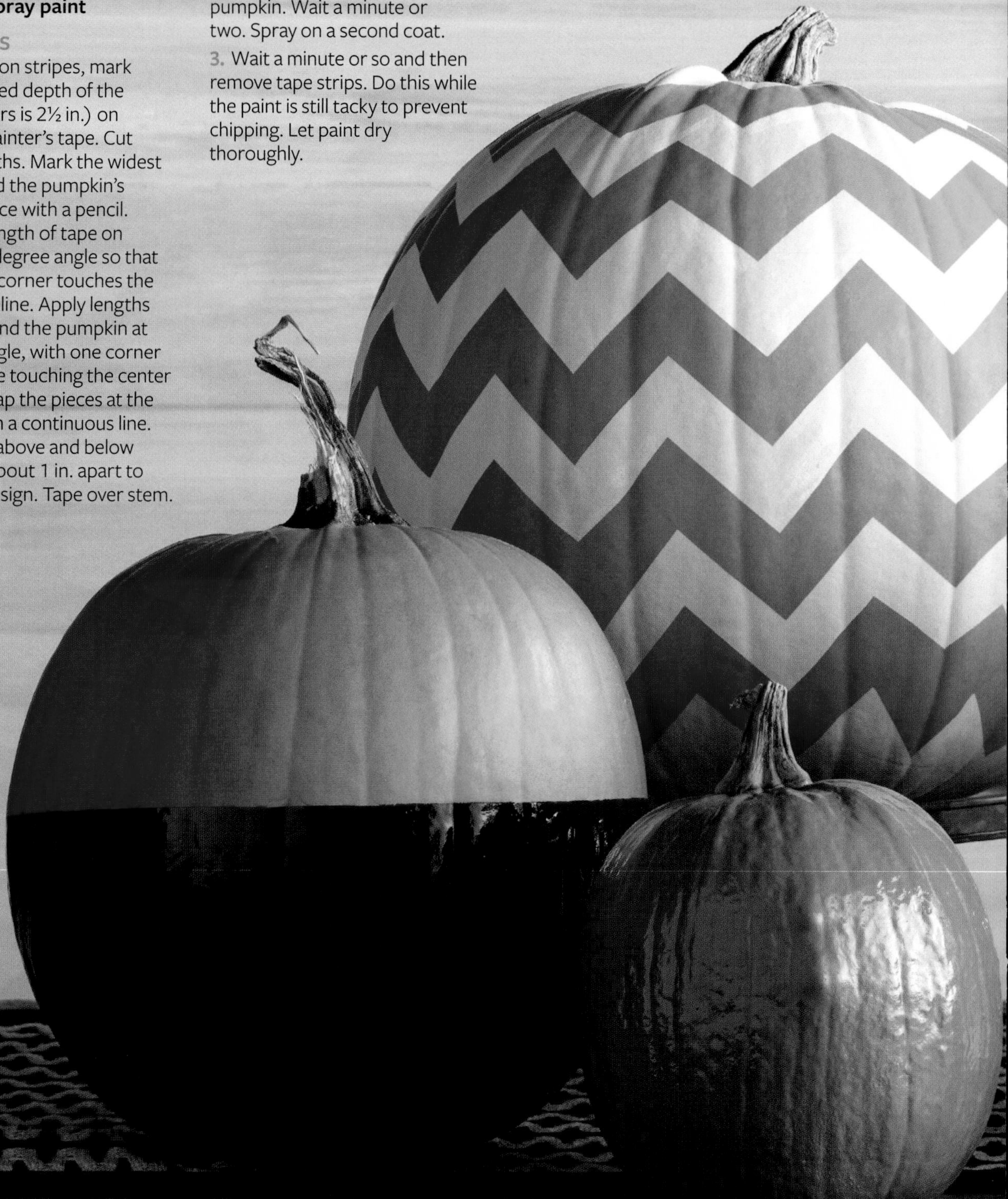

Front Yard Frights

Transform straw bales into scary-cool outdoor Halloween decorations with a few items from the hardware store.

WHAT YOU'LL NEED

3 straw bales
Spray paint in green, black and white
Craft foam sheets in green, black and white
Foam piping, black (½-in.)
Bendable aluminum rods (³⁄₁₆-in. diameter x .035 gauge)
Cheesecloth
Hot glue gun

DIRECTIONS

1. For all three creatures, spray-paint the straw bales first and let them dry. (If using two colors, let the first color dry before applying the next.)

2. Cut out the eyes and mouth from craft foam, and hot-glue them to the painted bales.

Ⓐ FRANKENSTEIN'S MONSTER

Spray-paint the lower three-quarters of straw bale green and the top one-quarter black. Add a scar of black craft foam. Make neck bolts by hot-gluing 2-in. lengths of foam piping to either side of the bale.

Ⓑ SPIDER

To get the leg length, start with a measuring tape at the top of the bale and unroll it in a curve, forming an arc to the ground. Cut six or eight lengths of foam piping to this measurement. Fit aluminum rods inside each leg, leaving 6-8 in. exposed at one end. Hot-glue rod to foam. Poke exposed rod end into top of the bale and curve each leg into position.

Ⓒ MUMMY

Wrap the bale in cheesecloth and hot-glue in place.

NOTES Straw bales can be decorated horizontally or vertically. Find bendable aluminum rods at a local hardware store.

Winter

Embrace the joys of new snow,
Christmas cheer and cozy times with family.

A sunset storm hovers over the
Nisqually Valley in Washington's
Mount Rainer National Park.
Photo by Mary Liz Austin

Yak cows enjoy
a sunny winter day.

Worth Yakking About

I hold my palm out flat and let the big guys eagerly gobble down their alfalfa treats. One gently pushes up against me, like a huge shaggy dog wanting to be petted.

"Do you want to sit on one?"

Jim Watson, who owns Spring Brook Ranch near Kalispell, Montana, with his wife, Carol Bibler, poses this question to me while we stand together in the pasture, surrounded by grunting Tibetan yaks.

My eyes grow wide and I manage a hesitant "OK." The yaks seem friendly—but they do have some pretty serious horns.

Before I can change my mind, Jim slips a halter on one and then gives me a leg up. The yak doesn't seem fazed, but this is definitely one of the most memorable moments in my agricultural journalism career.

The experience makes me curious to learn more. So I ask Jim to tell me the backstory.

He tells me that Carol's father, Sam Bibler, started buying and developing land for the ranch in the mid-1990s. The previous owners hadn't wanted it to be broken up into subdivisions, and they knew Sam was a conservation-minded buyer. The land—1,000 acres of native grass and timber just 35 miles from Glacier National Park—is now covered by a Montana Land Reliance easement that protects its agricultural value.

"We can farm, we can raise livestock. I have a small sawmill where I cut lumber for farm use, or I can do commercial logging, and have done so. There's not a conflict there at all," Jim says.

He compares the property to New York City's Central Park. "We're within a quarter-mile of the Kalispell city limits and have 50 neighbors that touch the property," he says.

"But we have elk and bears, eagles and hawks here. We love to see 'em, and part of our ranch management plan gives high priority to wildlife."

Sam started with bison after visiting broadcasting mogul Ted Turner's ranches and deciding the critters would do well on his own property. "Then he came across yaks and started buying them," Jim says.

"Unfortunately Sam passed away the next year, so he never got to see the calves."

Jim had no experience with yaks, but he grew up working with beef cattle, so he applied the same kind of animal husbandry methods with great success. In fact, if you ask him about the challenges of raising yaks, he can't really think of any. He says they're easier to raise than cattle, and far more interesting.

"They're smaller and more efficient, so you can stock more per acre. Yaks have shorter gestation and smaller calves. But they're quite robust and up running around right away, which goes back to their wild-animal instincts."

These descendants of sturdy, long-haired Himalayan beasts handle the Montana winters just fine: "Yaks are tough animals. We have nasty blizzards here, and they just lie down and let the snow cover them. You'll think they're gonna freeze to death, but it doesn't seem to affect them."

Temba (left), a Royal piebald yak, dashes through snow; Jim shares a snack with his buddies (right).

"One of the real benefits of owning yaks is being able to hang out with them."

Jim explains that Spring Brook's primary business is selling breeding stock. "We now consider ourselves one of the top, if not the premier, seed stock producers in the country. We're proud of what we do and have a very well-established breeding program."

The ranch also sells yak yarn and tanned hides, and its free-range, grass-fed meat is available in local specialty food stores and restaurants.

"There's a supply-demand problem," Jim says. "There aren't enough animals around to supply a large national grocery chain. But it's easy to sell the meat we have. It's tasty and healthy, and the prices are good."

One of the top criteria for breeding is personality. "We tell our customers that one of the real benefits of owning yaks is being able to hang out with them. You want animals that aren't flighty or aggressive."

Almost all the cows will come out when called to be petted, and they will eat out of your hand. "Pet cows tend to produce pet calves," Jim says. "We start working with them as soon as they're born."

The calves are weaned as a group and then put in the barn to get halter-trained so they become accustomed to people and to being handled. He credits Christy Novak, the ranch manager, for raising the yaks to be on their best behavior. "Christy is the yak tamer. She has a natural proclivity for communicating with animals, and they trust her."

"Yaks are much more intelligent than beef cattle, with richer personalities," Jim says. "If you treat them with kindness, they'll respond."

The big steers are his favorites. "They weigh half a ton, with impressive horns, but they just want treats and to get their backs scratched."

Goliath, a big, gentle steer with an injured knee, is the star of Spring Brook's school field trips. "We host a few hundred kids every spring," Jim says. "Goliath is so sweet that we let kids hug him and scratch his ears. We also let them climb up in the tractors and see the horses."

Jim loves the pace and variety of life on the ranch.

"Agriculture is good for people like me who get bored if there aren't a lot of things going on," he says. "It's slower in winter; we feed hay and fix up equipment, and Christy and I prepare for the National Western Stock Show in January. Then we calve in April, and the cycle starts over."

It's easy to see why he enjoys his job. I sure wouldn't mind hanging out here. In fact, I bet I'd have a very bright future as a professional yak rider.

Lori Vanover
Milwaukee, Wisconsin

Best Presents Ever!

The fun started early on Christmas morning. After my family finished opening presents, it was time to go outside and do chores before heading to Grandma's for dinner. Even though it was a holiday and really cold outside, work still had to be done.

Before I went outside, I gathered up all my wrapping paper, bows and ribbons and put my gifts in my room. I was about to throw the ribbons away when I got an idea. I grabbed a camera and walked down to the goat barn.

Inspired by the goats at our local county fair, I'd gotten two Nubian-Bohr females and a fainting female the previous year. (Yes, the fainting goat does faint.)

The first thing you need to know about goats is how and what to feed them. At the feed store, a bag caught my eye. The label said Sheep and Goat Feed. As I slung it over my shoulder, a man asked if I needed a cart. I said, "No, thank you, I've got it." It's amazing how many people give a girl a funny look when she's hauling a 50-pound bag of feed.

Along with feeding your goats, you also have to clip their nails, horns and hair. Breaking them to lead, too, can also be quite a challenge. For me, it took watching lots of YouTube videos—not to mention a visit from the fair's goat superintendent—before I finally got the hang of raising them.

Rewarding animals after you work with them lets them know they did a good job. I went up to the house and found a box of raisins. They loved them.

As I was doing other chores one day, I lost sight of my goats, then found them nibbling on Mom's flowers. I shooed them away, but they'd already eaten all the buds off her geraniums. I was afraid Mom would be upset with me, but she said it was OK. She didn't get many flowers that summer, though.

All my hard work paid off at the fair. We earned a few prizes, including Reserve Champion Dairy Goat, Champion Exotic Goat and three purple ribbons. That was exciting!

After the fair, I brought them home and bred them. The gestation period for goats is five months, so they should have kids toward the beginning of March—right around my birthday.

I've had so much fun with my goats, and as you can see by the photo, they were my best presents this Christmas!

Ashlynn Blenner
Holstein, Iowa

Ashlynn's goats show off their Christmas spirit.

Pat draws each year's angel design (left) and people send Christmas cards from the Village of Angelica, New York (above) with a cancellation like the one below.

The Miracle of Angel Station

In the tiny village of Angelica, New York, the post office is more than a place to get mail or send care packages. There you'll find the heart of this charming community. It's where residents meet and greet friends.

So when Angelica's post office was threatened with closure in the 1980s, resident Pat Kaake came up with a plan to save it. The village had already lost its school in favor of a modern building a few miles outside of town, and the nearest hospitals were 15 miles away in either direction.

In Pat's mind, it was paramount to keep a functioning post office. So she turned to the angels for help.

"At Christmastime I would hear on the news about towns named Snow or Bethlehem having celebrations," says Pat, who had moved to this tiny village from the big city. "I thought it was a wonderful idea, so I said, 'Why couldn't we do the same thing with Angelica?'"

Pat, who is an artist, created a postal cancellation design featuring an Angelica angel. Staying true to the nature of her adopted home, she drew her angels in a folksy fashion and submitted her proposal to the U.S. Postal Service. Once approved, the drawing was carved into a postmark cancellation stamp that could be used for one day only.

The postmistress at the time had another idea to make the day even more special and to further celebrate the spirit of Christmas—calling the post office Angel Station.

The massive uptick in mail volume saved Angelica's post office from closure and keeps the doors open today. Now it's tradition that on the first Friday in December, folks come to Angelica to mail their Christmas cards. People step through the door with its tinkling entrance bell and find the

December 4, 2015

Angel Station   Angelica, New York 14709

lobby decked with garlands, pine fronds and lights. A carved wooden angel flies near the ceiling. In the corner, a Christmas tree twinkles. Village supporters sit at tables that are topped with bowls of punch and platters of decorated cookies, offering hot chocolate or coffee to those who are mailing cards.

Each year the volume of mail going through the Angelica Post Office swells during late November and early December. Stamp collectors from around the world have embraced the Angel Station cancellation, some sending mail from as far away as France.

Because the stamp is destroyed each season, Pat draws a new angel that heralds season's greetings from Angel Station every year. Post offices may close in other parts of the country, but this tiny one endures, thanks to Pat and the miracle of Angel Station.

A.J. Sors
Wellsville, New York

Daddy's Little Farmhand

The door creaked when I opened it, the chill of the night softening as I stepped over the threshold and into the dimly lit barn on our Michigan farm. Through another door I heard the sound of milk hitting the bottom of the metal bucket that my father was using to milk Bossy.

I walked through the door, sat on a stool near my dad and began to do what I did best.

"Why do they call it 'the winter wonderland'?" I asked. I rambled on with other musings, never stopping long enough to hear a reply. As I talked, I watched the cats gathering expectantly around my father. The liquid made a rhythmic sound as his skillful milking quickly filled the bucket. Though the air in the stall had a winter chill, there was something warm about the moment. Like many farmers, my father had more to do than to say, so he continued to milk the cow while listening to his second-youngest daughter chatter away.

"We sure get a lot of milk from old Bossy, don't we, Daddy?" and "Those cats sure like it when you're milking!"

"If it keeps snowing like this, we might not have school tomorrow, huh, Daddy?" and "When is my sister coming home again?"

"Why didn't you ever sing with us, Daddy?" and "Are we going to take down the Christmas tree soon, Daddy?"

My father turned those milkers toward the cats again with a smile on his face. I watched in amusement as the cats licked the freshly squirted milk off of their fur, appreciating this rare playful act from my father. When the pail was nearly full, Daddy got up off the old milkin' stool. Because there was more to do and the night air was cold, he directed this young lady back to the house with the bucket.

"Oh, no! I'm supposed to help you with the chores, Daddy! Ma says I'm supposed to help you in the barn."

In such a moment the heart of a young child cannot possibly understand what goes through the mind of a father. He'd already worked a full day and just needed to get through the rigors of the after-supper chores. I knew nothing of my parents' financial pressures as Daddy waited to hear if he'd ever be called back to work. I didn't understand all that a day required of a mother

and father of eight. I only knew that my mother had called on me to help in the barn.

While carrying the weight of grown-up burdens, Daddy led me through the routine of scooping the corn feed and pulling apart another bale and distributing it to each of the cattle. He showed me how to collect the eggs so I didn't startle the chickens. I tried to act and feel grown up as I squeamishly followed my daddy's lead. With eggs and milk in tow, I was sent on my way through heavily falling snow toward the house.

As I trudged through knee-high snow, I regretted not listening to my mother, who told us kids to wrap our feet in old plastic bread bags so our socks and pants wouldn't get wet. I could feel the cold as the snow slowly melted and the wetness penetrated my jeans, which were tucked inside my boots.

Just inside the breezeway I put the milk pail on the top step and shouted, "Milk!" just as I'd heard my brothers do. I took my wet boots off and directed my musings toward my sisters. As they finished the dishes and pasteurized the milk, I listened as

they told me that Winter Wonderland was a state motto and that Daddy was much too busy to sing in our singing group.

Soon I was again out the door enjoying the evening snowfall with my siblings. As I peered up at the night sky, I saw the flakes fall toward and around me. They looked like little white planets racing by. I collected a large ball of snow and threw it at my brother, understanding that the farm in deep winter truly is a wonderland.

JoAnn Wegert
Elmore, Ohio

Like this busy little girl, JoAnn was eager to do chores in the family barn (pictured).

The Reliable Rocker

It was my go-to chair, the wooden rocker Tim and I got as a wedding present. I could have nicknamed it Loyal or Faithful.

I rocked all our babies in that chair, singing many lullabies and jingles, some of them composed on the spot as I attempted to sway the kids into slumber. That chair and I endured sleepless nights, sticky formula, baby spit-up, juice, Popsicles, runny noses and many breathing treatments.

Providing comfort and joy, the chair helped dry youthful tears. Many times the back-and-forth movement provided my only workout of the day as we read books, checked over homework or watched cartoons. Aging along with our family, the chair was ultimately tucked away in a spare bedroom to wait for grandchildren.

In 2011, when we sold our five-bedroom farmhouse and downsized, I sold the rocking chair to the new owners of our beloved home. *I don't have room for it anymore*, I told myself as I walked away.

About a year later, the young buyers held a garage sale. They must have discovered that the chair was a little wobbly (oops...I forgot to mention that) and were selling it. I looked it over for a long time, but the truth was I still didn't have a place for it, and they were charging more than I'd paid for it. *Way too expensive for a wobbly old chair*, I thought, running my fingers over its edges. *Walk away.*

At supper I told Tim about the chair. "You really want it, don't you?" he said. I reminded him that we needed to be sensible: Our limited space was the reason I'd sold it in the first place.

I started the dishes, and Tim, after a 10-hour workday, headed out to help one of our sons with a project. Much later, I was fast asleep when I heard my husband yelling, "Jamie, get out here!" His voice sounded tired and strained, and I wondered what might have happened.

When I got to the garage, I was relieved to see him smiling. And he had our chair! He also had quite the story. The garage sale was closed, and there was no answer at the door, but my dear, determined husband was on a mission. Tim went to the house where the owners' parents lived and knocked on their door. Excited to help, they were more than happy to open the garage and let him buy the chair.

I gave my husband a huge, tender hug. He looked so tired! I gently rubbed the worn, stained wood of the chair with the sleeve of my robe and said, "There are a lot of good memories in this chair, but I still don't know where we'll put it."

Tim grinned and whispered, "You'll find a place."

Then, heading into the house, he added, "Oh, by the way, did you know the thing is wobbly?"

"It is?" I replied. Oops...did I forget to mention that?

Jamie Klausing
Kalida, Ohio

Jamie lulled her children to sleep and comforted them in this rocking chair, which now sits on her front porch.

Baby Hayden's priceless expression shows exactly what Christmas is about in the eyes of a child.

Janelle Olson
Ithaca, Michigan

Last Christmas, Misty, our 3-month-old kitten, wouldn't leave the tree alone. Every time I heard her climbing it, I ran in, grabbed my camera, snapped a few pictures and then scolded her.

Shanna Arneson
Bozeman, Montana

Scrapbook

CAPTURE THE BEAUTY AROUND YOU

A wreath greets visitors to the Southern Star Covered Bridge near Suffield, Connecticut.
Photo by Paul Rezendes

"Nature is full of genius, full of the divinity; so that not a snowflake escapes its fashioning hand."

Henry David Thoreau

▲ This lovely sandhill crane thrilled me with its visit to my yard. I love the way its red mask stands out against the snowy background.

Renee Blake
Fenton, Michigan

▶ My brother and I shared a lot of good times on this sled when we were younger. My mother, Cathy, now uses it as a cheerful decoration during the holiday season.

Sara Thomas
Jonesville, Virginia

Little Landon helps his family find the perfect Christmas tree.

Vickie Saewert
Palmyra, Indiana

▲ I love the joy on my daughter Cecily's face as she tries to catch snowflakes.

Marianne Harris
Fruit Heights, Utah

▲ When Emmeline went sledding, her cousin's dog wanted to ride along, too.

Gail Seest
Mulberry, Indiana

Ryan sleds down the snow hill his dad thoughtfully piled up for him.

Photo by Damon & Tessa Satake, Dreaming Hollow Photography

► On a foggy day, our daughter Royce took a break from trailing cows to play with our dog, James. Her horse, Monty, wanted some attention, too.

Julie Verploegen
Havre, Montana

▲ During a terrible blizzard, I shot hundreds of photos and got some amazing lineups on the fence.

Carol Estes
La Porte, Indiana

► This birdhouse had been vacant for more than 10 years when a male red-shafted flicker moved in.

Cindy Haubert
Longmont, Colorado

"During the holiday season each of us thinks about someone we've loved and lost. Like the star of Bethlehem shone brightly to lead the world on a journey toward love, our own memories shine brighter at Christmas. That is the best present of all."

Sherrie Ball
Prairie du Chien, Wisconsin

I love driving through the country after a big snow to admire nature's beauty.
Jane Davis
Chetek, Wisconsin

◄ Early morning sunlight dances across the face of Mount Katahdin at Baxter State Park in Maine.

Photo by Paul Rezendes

▲ After an early dusting of snow, I captured this image at the Black Hills Wild Horse Sanctuary near Hot Springs, South Dakota.

Gerri Podrug
Hugo, Minnesota

▲ Two snowy white trumpeter swans were in the midst of a friendly fracas this winter day.

Cari Povenz
Grandville, Michigan

▶ These bluebirds huddled together for a long time, letting me get very close. They looked as eager for spring to arrive as I was!

Diane Johnston
Atoka, Tennessee

I found this funny face while enjoying the views from Cannon Mountain in New Hampshire's Franconia Notch State Park.

David Brownell
Madras, Oregon

All is calm as ice floats
along the surface of
this lake in Yellowstone
National Park.
Stephanie Noll
Pierre, South Dakota

A little ice makes an
ordinary dandelion
look extraordinary.
Linda Barnes
New London, Ohio

◀ For years we've put
a feeder and suet right
outside our sliding
glass doors so we can
catch glimpses of the
birds that come to eat,
especially in winter. One
of my favorites was this
friendly tufted titmouse,
just hanging out in the
snow and wind.

Noelle Sippel
Webster, New York

► A few Januarys ago, I made a trip to Davenport, Iowa, just to photograph the bald eagles on the Mississippi River. Watching them fish and seeing the skill they displayed was an absolutely amazing experience.

Mike Dickie
Adrian, Michigan

▲ A black-capped chickadee doesn't seem too bothered by the cold.

James Ridley
Brighton, Michigan

▲ This curious deer was scouting out our backyard before Christmas to help plan the best route for Santa's sleigh.

Betty McMillan
Wimbledon, North Dakota

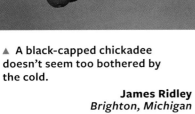

"Be tender with the young, compassionate with the aged, sympathetic with the striving and tolerant of the weak...someday in life you will have been all of these."

George Washington Carver

This rustic pole barn on our property took on a lovely glow at first light.
Jenny Gogel
Centennial, Colorado

▼ Birds will no doubt take shelter and a winter snack from this honeysuckle.
Norman Fairman
Perrysburg, Ohio

▲ A dusting of frost can't hide the beauty of this daisy.

Shelley Proude
Ottawa, Ontario

Early risers see an amazing view of Green Mountain National Forest. **Photo by Paul Rezendes**

All Is Calm, All Is Bright

Snow fell as I ran toward our red barn, telling two terriers, "Santa's coming, Santa's coming!" The dogs sensed my excitement and circled around me.

I was 7 years old that Christmas Eve in 1952, and as I did my chores on our Ohio farm I wondered if Santa would fix my sister Betty's old doll crib and buggy for me. Dad had sent them to Santa at the beginning of Advent.

I hope, I hope, I thought to myself as I rushed to the barn and plowed into Betty, who was carrying a straw bale for the calves.

"Watch where you're going!" she protested. "Why are you in such a hurry?" Then she smiled knowingly. "You know we can't go into the house until Santa turns on the Christmas tree lights and all the milking and feeding are done."

After I fed the calves, I cracked open the door of the barn and saw that night had come. A 40-watt bulb in the corner of the barn shed a faint light on the falling snow. The flakes drifted gently down, forming a misty curtain in front of the house.

My breathing slowed as I watched the snow fall. I wondered: *Jesus was born in a stable. Was there snow on His birthday? Did the animals keep Him warm with their breath and body heat? Jesus got gifts from the wise men. Did Santa do what Dad asked? Would I get my gifts?*

The barn seemed to breathe a response to my questions with the sounds of the calves rustling the straw, the rabbits thumping their hind legs and the cows lowing.

All of the ordinary sounds I heard every day became charged with the presence of something I couldn't name. I felt a sense of peace settling all around.

At that moment, the Christmas tree lights came on, the colors hazy through the falling snow. I stood entranced. I wanted to stay with that feeling of being part of it all. Presents? I would be happy with whatever I got.

My brother Dave looked out the door. "Hey, the lights are on! Jim and Betty have only four more cows to milk. Won't be long now. Come on!"

"Isn't everything beautiful, Dave? The snow, the lights, the barn?" Dave had already walked away and didn't hear me. "Yes, it is," I said softly.

Anticipation mounted as all four of us kids ran to the house. The Christmas tree's soft lights bathed the living room in a warm glow. Then I saw my gifts. The repainted doll crib and buggy; the new sheets in a flower design like the one on the sack our flour came in; matching pillowcases finished off with the crocheted edging Mom put on all her fancy work; my favorite doll with a new nightgown made of the same flannel as mine; and a dress and cap made of the same material as my school dress.

As I played with my doll and put her in her new bed, I saw my parents sitting on the couch, watching. They looked content. Again I felt the same presence as in the barn, only then I knew its name: love.

Marcia Dahlinghaus
Golden Valley, Arizona

Marcia (left, at age 6) waited in the big barn (right) as her siblings finished their chores on Christmas Eve.

'Boys Don't Ride Girls' Bikes'

I had never known a Christmas when we could ask for a special gift and actually expect to get it. The Great Depression of the 1930s was devastating to our farming community of Belleville, Michigan. Then came 1940; I was 7 years old and my brother, David, was 8. That year my father got a well-paying job, and the approaching holidays had a very different feeling. David and I were asked to choose the one gift we most wanted to get that year. I chose a teddy bear. David asked for a bicycle.

The anticipation of Christmas morning became almost unbearable. Every day I pestered David with the same question: "Do you really think we'll get what we asked for?"

Every day he'd answer the same way: "How do I know?"

Then that wonderful morning arrived. There under the tree, with a big red bow around his neck, was my teddy bear. David's bicycle, however, was not there. I wondered how my parents could grant my wish but not my brother's.

"I forgot something," my father said, as he went into the other room. When he came back he was pushing a bicycle.

On David's face was a look of both disappointment and delight. The bike was secondhand, which David didn't mind, but it was a girls' bike. Boys did not ride girls' bikes. Personally, I wouldn't have cared if it had come with pink bows—it was still a bicycle. That marvelous two-wheeled invention represented freedom to David and me. Even if I only rode on the handlebars, it would give us mobility.

David and I had been learning to ride on bicycles borrowed from friends in the neighborhood. I was not as accomplished a rider as he was, but I could manage to get from point A to point B without too many mishaps. Since he didn't have to ride his Christmas bike to school, David avoided being teased about the fact that it wasn't a boys' bike. And he was never teased about it in our neighborhood because David was bigger than most of the other kids.

My brother was very generous, letting me ride his new wheels often. He even figured out a way to tie our Radio Flyer wagon to the bike so he could pull me and other kids up and down our road.

Now we could explore places that were once beyond convenient walking distance. That winter we took many long rides down the snowy back roads, with me perched on the handlebars or riding behind in the wagon. That bicycle truly gave us an exciting new freedom.

Daniel Burch Fiddler
Fort Bragg, California

David towed Daniel and their friends all over the neighborhood on his secondhand girls' bike.

An Old Secret Still Shines

Just before Christmas, my daughter Katie and I went over to my dad's place to decorate. While we worked, grandbabies Decie and Johnny entertained their great-grandfather Papa Cox.

Their laughter and occasional squabbles must have reminded Papa of when my brother and I were just their size, because I saw a twinkle in his 80-year-old eyes.

While hanging the familiar ornaments on Papa's tree, I couldn't help gently caressing the very oldest of the glass balls. Those I made sure to suspend from the uppermost branches, safely out of reach of tiny hands.

When the tree was beautifully dressed and glowing, we bid my dad goodbye with lots of hugs and kisses and headed for home. Later that night, in the quiet darkness, I pulled my memories up close and snuggled down to rest and remember.

The Christmas of my 16th year, while decorating the tree with Mama, I accidentally dropped and broke an ornament. The glass ball was blue and peeling; it had been on our tree for as long as I could remember.

Ruefully, I knelt to pick up the shattered pieces and was surprised to find a small slip of paper among the shards. Unfolding the tiny note, I recognized my dad's crudely penciled writing. Lifting my eyes, I saw my mother's fond expression.

"Your daddy wrote that and stuck it in the blue ball during our first Christmas together, just before you were born," she said with a smile.

I wouldn't have believed it, except for the proof there in my hands. The daddy I knew always looked upon getting the tree decorated as a chore he wanted little part in. In fact, sometimes he could be a bit of a Scrooge around the holidays! And yet this bit of yellowed paper proved that long ago my daddy had done something downright romantic at Christmas.

Carefully laying the note aside, I cleaned up the shattered fragments, wishing I could reassemble the pieces somehow. "It's OK," Mama said, reassuring me with a hug. "Just pick out another of the old ones and tuck the note back inside."

Now, as we celebrate the holidays without Mama, who we lost to cancer, my discovery becomes more poignant. Each year as I decorate Papa's tree, I relive the moment I shared with her that winter afternoon and blink away a tear.

As I carefully handle those old ornaments, I love knowing that one holds a secret between Papa and Mama—a secret that was obvious to all who knew them.

The note inside one of those glass balls on Papa's tree holds the heart of my parents' marriage in three little words: "I love you."

Lois Marie Guymer
Jacksonville, Texas

The Holiday Rush

I worked lots of extra hours my first Christmas season as a clerk for Dancer's, the department store in my small hometown of Wayland, Michigan.

I'd started the job, which paid 85 cents an hour, that summer of 1966 after getting a work permit at the age of 15. Our neighbor Arnie Wilde was the shop manager, and I soon learned how to fit shoes, measure and cut cloth, and keep the shelves of shirts and underwear nice and neat.

We closed at 6 p.m. on Christmas Eve, and at 5:55, a local farmer came in to find gifts for his wife. Arnie told me this was a holiday habit of Mr. Johnson's, and that we'd do our best to take care of him.

I knew Mr. Johnson, whose daughter was in my class and in the band, so I went to help him. We wandered through the sweaters, dresses and skirts, the pretty towels and practical flannel nightgowns. We talked about size and color and what I thought Mrs. Johnson would like. After nearly half an hour of mulling, Mr. Johnson decided on a flannel nightgown with pretty pink fuzzy slippers to match and a piece of jewelry that I'd pointed out to him. I wrapped his gifts and completed the sale, and Arnie and I walked home for dinner.

The next Christmas Eve, like clockwork, Mr. Johnson came in at 5:55. We went through the same process, taking lots of time again to choose and wrap gifts. Tired but happy, Arnie and I headed for home.

By my third Christmas at the department store, I was an experienced salesclerk. Mrs. Johnson had come into the store in late summer to buy school clothes for the kids, and we visited while I helped her shop. As she commented on pretty colors and the lovely way a dress was made, I made mental notes.

When Mr. Johnson made his last-minute appearance on Christmas Eve, I was ready. I told him, "Mrs. Johnson was in not too long ago, and I noticed how much she liked this royal blue sweater and the plaid skirt that goes with it so beautifully."

She'd also told me that she really needed new boots, confiding that she was ashamed to walk into church with her old ones.

I'd found some perfect boots in her size and had put them aside for Christmas Eve. Well, Mr. Johnson was impressed, and I think more than a little relieved. We had him out the door by 6:10 with everything wrapped in paper and ribbons!

I worked for three more holiday seasons and was always there just before closing on Christmas Eve, when Mr. Johnson knew I had the answers he needed. Sure, the big stores in Grand Rapids had more items to choose from and lovely Christmas fantasies in their windows, but it's only in a small town that neighbors take care of each other.

Patti Clark
Concord, California

In a small town, residents hustle to find the perfect gift on Christmas Eve.

Tending to a calf on Christmas Eve reminded Jack of Jesus' humble birthplace.

A Calf for Christmas

With no electricity on our farm just north of Charleston, Illinois, Christmas Eve 1940 was far different than it is today. The holiday didn't affect the dairy cows, which still had to be milked by hand, and often we had to chop ice in the water troughs so the cattle could drink. Sometimes we had to perform gymnastics in the snow or on the ice just to get bales of hay and grain to the animals.

We went to church that night in a drafty old car with an anemic heater and an engine that was reluctant to start at much below 20 degrees. Over our good clothes we wore heavy coats, gloves and hats.

Just 5 years old, I was excited to have a part in the children's pageant. With the church dressed in its finest and all our favorite old hymns ringing out, each of us felt the joy of the Christ Child's birth in our hearts.

Back home, as we turned on the kerosene lamps in the living room, I contemplated the arrival of Santa Claus. Around 8:30, Dad told Mother he was going to look in on a cow that was due to calve at any time. Always eager to see a little calf, I found an excuse to go along.

Putting on my winter wear, I waited while Dad lit a kerosene lantern. He took my small hand in his as we headed toward the barn. A bright moon shone down,

and our steps squeaked in the heavy snow. As we opened the barn door, the familiar, agreeable smells of cured clover hay and cattle greeted us.

The dim light revealed a new heifer calf on a pile of straw next to her mother. Dad seemed pleased to have a Christmas calf and was in a mood to reminisce.

He related a childhood story: that at midnight on Christmas Eve, all the cattle would lie facedown in the manger as if bowing before Baby Jesus. I asked if he'd ever gone to the barn at midnight to see it. He never had, but allowed that it certainly could be true.

As we returned to the warmth of the house, I pondered Dad's story and other mysterious things, like why Santa never left tracks in the snow. I secretly vowed to return to the barn at midnight. Of course, I never made it, being far off in dreamland when the clock struck 12.

As I grew, I solved the mystery of Santa, but another Christmas mystery remains: that God's son was born in a most humble and unlikely place, that he was sent to save someone like me, and that God expected no payment from me greater than simple obedience to His word. Now, that's a real mystery.

Jack Pierce
Mattoon, Illinois

A band of horses looks for forage in the snow on Colorado's Wild Horse Mesa.

Kindred Spirits

A band of horses was milling about in Judy Barnes' front yard when I drove up. The ground below their hooves was pulverized—a sign of constant activity. A strong wind lifted clouds of soil into the air and ruffled the heavy winter coats of these wild creatures. They were hungry, waiting for a handful of hay.

Then Judy, dressed warmly to ward off the frigid air of this January day, emerged from her two-story cabin. A bay mare with her foal edged forward to greet her; the rest of the group followed cautiously.

"This mare foaled here in my yard late last spring," Judy said as we walked toward a weather-beaten tramp shed a few minutes from her cabin. In one corner sat a meager supply of hay protected by a barricade and a gate. While cutting the strings of one of the bales and pitching slices to the hungry four-legged crowd, Judy explained that she was waiting for more donations of hay to come in.

Judy is a former city girl and professional photographer who has loved horses all her life. Ten years ago she found a simple homestead on Wild Horse Mesa, a marginally populated desert community covering 75 square miles in south-central Colorado. She had heard about the wild horses and wanted to live among them, with plans to photograph and write a book about them. Her cabin is

Judy knows many of the animals that live on Wild Horse Mesa and has named a few, including this white horse, Casanova.

off the electric grid; a few solar panels provide power and a woodstove is the main source of heat. Winters are rough, and serious shopping is hours away.

A year after moving to Colorado, Judy started Spirit of the Wild Horse, a foundation dedicated to helping these animals survive. She estimates that roughly 150 mustangs roam the 25,000-acre mesa, which is mostly private land. I had heard about Judy through a friend and wanted to pitch in, so I tagged along on this brisk day to help her feed the horses.

"I adopted five wild horses when I moved here," Judy told me. "One of the mares was over 35 years old and bred. I named her Esperanza. I lost her to old age two years later."

Esperanza was a fitting name for this wild creature, a descendant of the horses brought to the Southwest by the Spanish conquistadors around 1500. Escaped horses soon multiplied, formed individual bands and began roaming the open range.

With horses moving around us, we loaded the last of the square bales into the rear of Judy's battered pickup and secured the open end with bungee cords. The tailgate was missing. "It fell off the other day," she explained. "I'm waiting on parts."

Off we went over rutted dirt roads curving through what appeared to be a never-ending mesa, where sage and rabbit brush dominated the landscape. The snow-covered peaks of the Sangre de Cristo, La Garita and San Juan ranges sparkled all around us.

"This country grows on you," Judy said. "I wouldn't want to live anywhere else."

We traveled the back roads for several hours, not once passing another vehicle, always on the lookout for small bands of horses. We focused on arroyos or scarcely populated stands of pinons and junipers, places where horses sometimes take refuge from the wind. Judy knows her feeding spots and all the animals. She's even named some of them.

Life isn't easy for man or beast on the mesa. A small water tank below Judy's cabin serves as a poor substitute for a stock pond. And since she has no well, she pays to have water trucked in for her needs and those of the horses.

To fund her foundation, Judy sells photographs of the horses and gives tours of the area for a fee. Though some generous folks have donated hay, Judy sometimes has to buy forage herself. It's a struggle to care for the animals. She is raising money to buy 300 acres with a well so the horses have a place to graze and drink water.

When our day together was over, I couldn't help but be impressed by Judy's dedication to the horses. She has come to this high desert and found kindred spirits among the creatures she loves.

Karin Deneke
Fort Garland, Colorado

When Everything Was Priority Mail

Licking hundreds of stamps for other folks' cards was a Christmas tradition in the Hess family.

Every Christmas, Harry "Pat" Hess' family would become unpaid employees of the post office.
Postage at the time was 2 cents an ounce, but farm families around New Lothrop and Maple Grove, Michigan, often couldn't get to town to buy stamps. When Pat, our mailman, collected hundreds of unstamped Christmas cards from the boxes on his rural route—along with piles of pennies for postage—it became a tremendous job to stamp everything. So each night his kids sat around the kitchen table licking stamps.

Pat, like fellow carrier Hiram Walter, went above and beyond for his customers. In response to many a note left in mailboxes, he often delivered groceries, drugs and other emergency supplies—even harness parts—when a busy farmer couldn't take time for a trip to town. He'd pick up what was needed and then drop off the parcels on the next day's rounds.

Such tasks were a big challenge in the early years of his route, which began in 1910 when Pat covered 12 miles with a pack on his back. In time he went to a horse and buggy, and there were days when farmers had to use a team of horses to pull him over muddy roads.

Each day he started with one horse, covered about half his route, stopped at home for dinner and changed horses. Then, as he finished his rounds, he got out of the buggy and walked the last 2 miles so the tired horse wouldn't have to pull him.

He kept lighted lanterns beneath blankets in the buggy to keep his feet from freezing in the months when he started out long before daylight and came home by moonlight. Then he warmed up by doing a couple of hours of chores on his farm.

When I was a young girl growing up in the 1940s, I also entrusted my two pennies for postage to our mail carrier. Usually it was for letters responding to offers of free merchandise that I'd clip from newspapers, magazines or cereal boxes. It brought excitement to a farm girl's day to wait for something like the greeting

Harry "Pat" Hess (right) continued a long tradition of high-quality postal service begun by New Lothrop's first mail carriers (below, from left), Venus Wilson and Cyrus Judd, seen when the routes were established, sometime in 1905.

card samples I once received. With my trusty bicycle I earned enough money selling boxes of cards to buy my mom—and myself, too—our first electric mixer.

For all 41 years of Pat's rural route, postage for a first-class stamp was either 2 or 3 cents an ounce. It wasn't till six years after his 1952 retirement that the rate went up to 4 cents. We all agreed Pat wouldn't have stood for such a thing!

Janet Ruddy
New Lothrop, Michigan

Mushroom & Leek Strudel

PREP: 50 MIN. + COOLING
BAKE: 20 MIN. + STANDING
MAKES: 2 STRUDELS (12 SLICES EACH)

INGREDIENTS

- 2 tablespoons butter, divided
- 2 pounds fresh mushrooms, finely chopped, divided
- 1 medium leek (white portion only), chopped, divided
- 2 garlic cloves, minced
- ¼ cup white wine
- ¼ cup heavy whipping cream
- 2 tablespoons minced fresh parsley
- 1 tablespoon minced fresh thyme or 1 teaspoon dried thyme
- ½ teaspoon salt
- ¼ teaspoon pepper

ASSEMBLY
- 12 sheets phyllo dough (14x9 inches)
- ¾ cup butter, melted
- 4 tablespoons grated Parmesan cheese, divided

DIRECTIONS

1. In a large skillet, heat 1 tablespoon butter over medium-high heat. Add half each of mushrooms and leek. Cook and stir until mushrooms are lightly browned and leek is tender; remove from pan. Repeat with remaining butter, mushrooms and leek, adding garlic during the last minute of cooking. Return all to pan.
2. Stir in wine and cream; cook 1-2 minutes or until liquid is almost evaporated. Stir in herbs, salt and pepper. Remove from pan; cool completely.
3. Preheat oven to 375°. Place one sheet of phyllo dough on a work surface; brush with butter. Layer with five additional phyllo sheets, brushing each layer. (Keep remaining phyllo covered with plastic wrap and a damp towel to prevent it from drying out.)
4. Spoon half of the mushroom mixture down center third of phyllo dough to within 1 in. of ends. Sprinkle filling with 2 tablespoons cheese. Fold up short sides to enclose filling. Roll up jelly-roll style, starting with a long side.
5. Transfer to a parchment paper-lined 15x10x1-in. baking pan, seam side down. Brush with additional butter. Repeat with remaining ingredients. Bake 18-22 minutes or until golden brown.
6. Let stand 10 minutes before slicing. Serve warm.

Jolly Ginger Reindeer Cookies

PREP: 50 MIN. + CHILLING • **BAKE:** 10 MIN./BATCH + COOLING • **MAKES:** ABOUT 4 DOZEN

INGREDIENTS

- ½ cup butter, softened
- 1 cup packed brown sugar
- 1 large egg
- ¾ cup molasses
- 3½ cups all-purpose flour
- 2 teaspoons ground ginger
- 1 teaspoon baking powder
- 1 teaspoon baking soda
- 1 teaspoon ground cinnamon
- 1 teaspoon ground allspice

ROYAL ICING

- 2 cups confectioners' sugar
- 2 tablespoon plus 2 tsp. water
- 4 teaspoons meringue powder
- ¼ teaspoon cream of tartar
- 1 to 2 tablespoons miniature semisweet chocolate chips
- 1 to 2 tablespoon Red Hots

DIRECTIONS

1. In a large bowl, cream butter and brown sugar until light and fluffy. Beat in egg and molasses. In another bowl, whisk flour, ginger, baking powder, baking soda, cinnamon and allspice; gradually beat into creamed mixture.

2. Divide dough in half. Shape each into a disk; wrap disks in plastic. Refrigerate 1 hour or until firm enough to roll.

3. Preheat oven to 350°. On a lightly floured surface, roll each portion of dough to ¼-in. thickness. Cut with a floured 3-in. gingerbread boy-shaped cookie cutter. Place 1 in. apart on greased baking sheets.

4. Bake 10-12 minutes or until set. Cool on pans 1 minute. Remove to wire racks to cool completely.

5. In a bowl, combine confectioners' sugar, water, meringue powder and cream of tartar; beat on low just until blended. Beat on high for 4-5 minutes or until stiff peaks form. Keep the unused icing covered at all times with a damp cloth. If necessary, beat again on high speed to restore texture.

6. To decorate, place cookies on a work surface with heads facing you. Pipe antlers onto legs. With icing, attach chocolate chips for eyes and Red Hots for noses. Let stand to set.

Praline-Topped Apple Bread

PREP: 30 MIN. • **BAKE:** 50 MIN. + COOLING
MAKES: 1 LOAF (16 SLICES)

INGREDIENTS

- 2 cups all-purpose flour
- 2 teaspoons baking powder
- ½ teaspoon baking soda
- ½ teaspoon salt
- 1 cup sugar
- 1 cup (8 ounces) sour cream
- 2 large eggs
- 3 teaspoons vanilla extract
- 1½ cups chopped peeled Granny Smith apples
- 1¼ cups chopped pecans, toasted, divided
- ½ cup butter, cubed
- ½ cup packed brown sugar

DIRECTIONS

1. Preheat oven to 350°. In a large bowl, mix flour, baking powder, baking soda and salt. In another bowl, beat the sugar, sour cream, eggs and vanilla until well blended. Stir into the flour mixture just until moistened. Fold in apples and 1 cup pecans.
2. Transfer batter to a greased 9x5-in. loaf pan. Bake for 50-55 minutes or until a toothpick inserted in center comes out clean. Cool in pan 10 minutes. Remove to a wire rack to cool completely.
3. In a small saucepan, combine butter and brown sugar. Bring to a boil, stirring constantly to dissolve the sugar; boil 1 minute. Spoon over bread. Sprinkle with remaining pecans; let stand until set.

Risotto Balls (Arancini)

PREP: 35 MIN. • **BAKE:** 25 MIN.
MAKES: ABOUT 3 DOZEN

INGREDIENTS

- 1½ cups water
- 1 cup uncooked arborio rice
- 1 teaspoon salt
- 2 large eggs, lightly beaten
- ⅔ cup sun-dried tomato pesto
- 2 cups panko (Japanese) bread crumbs, divided
  Marinara sauce, warmed

DIRECTIONS

1. Preheat oven to 375°. In a large saucepan, combine water, rice and salt; bring to a boil. Reduce heat; simmer, covered, 18-20 minutes or until the liquid is absorbed and rice is tender. Let stand, covered, 10 minutes. Transfer to a large bowl; cool slightly. Add eggs and pesto; stir in 1 cup bread crumbs.
2. Place remaining bread crumbs in a shallow bowl. Shape rice mixture into 1¼-in. balls. Roll in bread crumbs, patting to help coating adhere. Place on greased 15x10x1-in. baking pans. Bake 25-30 minutes or until golden brown. Serve with marinara sauce.

Lemon Meltaways

PREP: 15 MIN. + CHILLING
BAKE: 10 MIN./BATCH + COOLING

INGREDIENTS

- ¾ cup butter, softened
- ⅓ cup confectioners' sugar
- 1 teaspoon lemon juice
- 1¼ cups all-purpose flour
- ½ cup cornstarch

FROSTING

- ¼ cup butter, softened
- ¾ cup confectioners' sugar
- 1 teaspoon grated lemon zest
- 1 teaspoon lemon juice
- 1 to 3 drops yellow food coloring, optional

DIRECTIONS

1. In a bowl, beat butter and confectioners' sugar until blended. Beat in lemon juice. In a small bowl, whisk flour and cornstarch; gradually beat into butter mixture. Divide dough in half; shape each into an 8-in.-long roll. Wrap in plastic; refrigerate 2 hours or until firm.
2. Preheat oven to 350°. Unwrap and cut cookie dough crosswise into ¼-in. slices. Place 2 in. apart on ungreased baking sheets.
3. Bake 8-12 minutes or until firm. Remove from pans to wire racks to cool completely.
4. For the frosting, in a small bowl, beat butter and confectioners' sugar until smooth. Beat in lemon zest, lemon juice and, if desired, food coloring. Spread over cooled cookies.

Melting Snowman

PREP: 10 MIN. + FREEZING
MAKES: 1 DOZEN

INGREDIENTS

- ¾ cup whipped topping
  - Miniature semisweet chocolate chips
  - Orange jimmies
  - Hot cocoa

DIRECTIONS

Using a small cookie scoop, shape snowmen by dropping 1-tablespoon portions of whipped topping onto a waxed paper-lined baking sheet. Decorate with chocolate chips and jimmies to create faces. Freeze until firm. Place over servings of hot cocoa just before serving.

Loaded Baked Potato Dip

START TO FINISH: 10 MIN.
MAKES: 2½ CUPS

INGREDIENTS

- 2 cups (16 ounces) reduced-fat sour cream
- 2 cups shredded reduced-fat cheddar cheese
- 8 center-cut bacon or turkey bacon strips, chopped and cooked
- ⅓ cup minced fresh chives
- 2 teaspoons Louisiana-style hot sauce
   Hot cooked waffle-cut fries

DIRECTIONS

In a small bowl, mix the first five ingredients until blended; refrigerate until serving. Serve with waffle fries.

Favorite Cheesy Potatoes

PREP: 30 MIN. • **BAKE:** 45 MIN.
MAKES: 12 SERVINGS (⅔ CUP EACH)

INGREDIENTS

- 3½ pounds potatoes (about 7 medium), peeled and cut into ¾-inch cubes
- 1 can (10½ ounces) condensed cream of potato soup, undiluted
- 1 cup French onion dip
- ¾ cup 2% milk
- ⅔ cup sour cream
- 1 teaspoon minced fresh parsley
- ¼ teaspoon salt
- ¼ teaspoon pepper
- 1 package (16 ounces) process cheese (Velveeta), cubed
  Additional minced fresh parsley

DIRECTIONS

1. Preheat oven to 350°. Place potatoes in a Dutch oven; add water to cover. Bring to a boil. Reduce heat; cook, uncovered, 8-12 minutes or until tender. Drain. Cool slightly.
2. In a large bowl, mix soup, onion dip, milk, sour cream, parsley, salt and pepper; gently fold in potatoes and cheese. Transfer to a greased 13x9-in. baking dish.
3. Bake, covered, 30 minutes. Uncover; bake 15-20 minutes longer or until heated through and cheese is melted. Just before serving, stir to combine and sprinkle with additional parsley. (Potatoes will thicken upon standing.)

Black-Eyed Peas & Ham

PREP: 20 MIN. + SOAKING • **COOK:** 5 HOURS
MAKES: 12 SERVINGS (¾ CUP EACH)

INGREDIENTS

- 1 package (16 ounces) dried black-eyed peas, rinsed and sorted
- ½ pound fully cooked boneless ham, finely chopped
- 1 medium onion, finely chopped
- 1 medium sweet red pepper, finely chopped
- 5 bacon strips, cooked and crumbled
- 1 large jalapeno pepper, seeded and finely chopped
- 2 garlic cloves, minced
- 1½ teaspoons ground cumin
- 1 teaspoon reduced-sodium chicken bouillon granules
- ½ teaspoon salt
- ½ teaspoon cayenne pepper
- ¼ teaspoon pepper
- 6 cups water
  Minced fresh cilantro, optional
  Hot cooked rice

DIRECTIONS

Soak peas according to package directions. Transfer peas to a 6-qt. slow cooker; add the next 12 ingredients. Cover and cook on low 5-7 hours or until peas are tender. Sprinkle with cilantro if desired. Serve with rice.

Gingerbread Hazelnut Biscotti

PREP: 30 MIN. + STANDING • **COOK:** 35 MIN. + COOLING

INGREDIENTS

- 1¾ cups all-purpose flour
- ¾ cup packed dark brown sugar
- 1 teaspoon baking powder
- ¾ teaspoon ground cinnamon
- ½ teaspoon ground ginger
- ½ teaspoon baking soda
- ½ teaspoon kosher salt
- ⅛ teaspoon ground cloves
- 1 cup old-fashioned oats, divided
- 2 large eggs
- ¼ cup molasses
- 2 tablespoons canola oil
- ½ teaspoon vanilla extract
- ¾ cup coarsely chopped hazelnuts, toasted
- ¾ cup raisins

DRIZZLE
- ¼ cup white baking chips
- ½ teaspoon shortening

DIRECTIONS

1. Preheat oven to 350°. In a large bowl, whisk the first eight ingredients. Place ½ cup oats in a food processor; cover and process until ground. Stir remaining oats and ground oats into flour mixture. In a small bowl, whisk eggs, molasses, oil and vanilla; gradually beat into flour mixture. Stir in chopped hazelnuts and raisins (the dough will be thick).
2. Divide dough in half. Using lightly floured hands, shape each into a 12x2-in. rectangle on parchment paper-lined baking sheets. Bake 25-30 minutes or until a toothpick inserted in center comes out clean. Cool on pans on wire racks 8-10 minutes or until firm.
3. Transfer baked rectangles to a cutting board. Using a serrated knife, cut diagonally into ¾-in. slices. Return to baking sheets, cut side down.
4. Bake 5-6 minutes on each side or until firm. Remove from pans to wire racks to cool completely.
5. In a microwave, melt baking chips and shortening; stir until smooth. Drizzle over biscotti; let stand until set. Store between pieces of waxed paper in airtight containers.

Hazelnut Mocha Coffee

PREP: 5 MIN. • **COOK:** 10 MIN. + CHILLING
MAKES: 6 SERVINGS

INGREDIENTS

- 4 ounces semisweet chocolate, chopped
- 1 cup heavy whipping cream
- ⅓ cup sugar
- ½ teaspoon ground cinnamon
- 2 tablespoons hazelnut liqueur
- 4½ cups hot brewed coffee
  Sweetened whipped cream, optional

DIRECTIONS

1. Place chocolate in a small bowl. In a small saucepan, bring cream just to a boil. Add sugar and cinnamon; cook and stir until sugar is dissolved. Pour over chocolate; stir with a whisk until smooth. Stir in liqueur.
2. Cool to room temperature, stirring occasionally. Refrigerate, covered, until cold. Beat just until soft peaks form, about 15 seconds (do not overbeat). For each serving, spoon ¼ cup into mugs. Top with ¾ cup coffee; stir to dissolve. Top with whipped cream if desired.

Chocolate-Drizzled Gingerbread
PREP: 25 MIN. • **BAKE:** 40 MIN. + COOLING • **MAKES:** 9 SERVINGS

INGREDIENTS
- ½ cup butter, softened
- ½ cup packed brown sugar
- 1 large egg
- ½ cup molasses
- 1¾ cups all-purpose flour
- 1 teaspoon baking powder
- ½ teaspoon ground ginger
- ¼ teaspoon salt
- ⅛ teaspoon ground cloves
- ½ cup water
- 4 ounces bittersweet chocolate, melted and slightly cooled

TOPPING
- ¾ cup heavy whipping cream
- 2 tablespoons confectioners' sugar
- ¼ teaspoon ground ginger
  Chopped crystallized ginger and chocolate shavings, optional

DIRECTIONS
1. Preheat oven to 325°. In a large bowl, cream butter and brown sugar until light and fluffy. Add egg, then molasses, beating well after each addition.
2. In another bowl, mix flour, baking powder, ground ginger, salt and cloves; gradually add to creamed mixture alternately with water, beating well after each addition.
3. Pour half of the batter into a greased 8-in. square baking dish. Drizzle with half of the melted chocolate. Top with remaining batter and melted chocolate. Bake 40-45 minutes or until a toothpick inserted in the center comes out clean. Cool completely on a wire rack.
4. For topping, in a small bowl, beat cream until it begins to thicken. Add confectioners' sugar and ginger; beat until soft peaks form. Serve with cake. If desired, sprinkle with crystallized ginger and chocolate shavings.

Crab Cakes with Peanut Sauce

PREP: 25 MIN. + CHILLING • **COOK:** 5 MIN./BATCH
MAKES: 1 DOZEN (⅓ CUP SAUCE)

INGREDIENTS
- ¼ cup rice vinegar
- 2 tablespoons creamy peanut butter
- 1 garlic clove, minced
- 1 teaspoon brown sugar
- 1 teaspoon olive oil
- ¼ teaspoon ground mustard
- Dash cayenne pepper

CRAB CAKES
- 1 cup plain Greek yogurt
- ⅔ cup crushed saltines (about 15 crackers)
- ¼ cup finely chopped celery
- ¼ cup finely chopped roasted sweet red pepper
- ¼ cup minced fresh parsley
- 2 tablespoons finely chopped onion
- 1 large egg white, lightly beaten
- 1 tablespoon fresh lemon juice
- 2 teaspoons prepared horseradish
- ½ teaspoon paprika
- ¼ teaspoon salt
- 1 pound lump crabmeat, drained
- 1 tablespoon olive oil
- Minced fresh chives

DIRECTIONS
1. In a small bowl, whisk the first seven ingredients until blended. Set aside.
2. In a large bowl, mix the first 11 crab cake ingredients until blended. Fold in crab. Shape into twelve ½-in.-thick patties. Refrigerate, covered, 30 minutes.
3. In a large skillet, heat 1 tablespoon oil over medium-high heat. Add crab cakes in batches; cook 2-3 minutes on each side or until golden brown. Sprinkle with fresh chives; serve with sauce.

Pear Cider

PREP: 5 MIN. • **COOK:** 3 HOURS
MAKES: 20 SERVINGS (¾ CUP EACH)

INGREDIENTS
- 12 cups unsweetened apple juice
- 4 cups pear nectar
- 8 cinnamon sticks (3 inches)
- 1 tablespoon whole allspice
- 1 tablespoon whole cloves

DIRECTIONS
1. In a 6-qt. slow cooker, combine juice and nectar. Place the cinnamon sticks, allspice and cloves on a double thickness of cheesecloth; bring up corners of cloth and tie with string to form a bag. Place in slow cooker.
2. Cover and cook on low for 3-4 hours or until heated through. Discard spice bag. Serve warm cider in mugs.

Zippy Sirloin Steak

PREP: 15 MIN. + MARINATING • **GRILL:** 20 MIN.
MAKES: 6 SERVINGS

INGREDIENTS

- 1 tablespoon paprika
- 2 teaspoons pepper
- 1½ teaspoons kosher salt
- 1½ teaspoons brown sugar
- 1½ teaspoons ground cumin
- 1½ teaspoons chili powder
- 1 teaspoon sugar
- ¼ teaspoon cayenne pepper
- 1 beef sirloin tip steak (1½ pounds)

DIRECTIONS

1. In a small bowl, combine the first eight ingredients. Rub over both sides of beef. Cover and refrigerate for 2 hours.

2. On a lightly greased grill rack, grill the beef, covered, over medium heat or broil 4 in. from the heat 8-10 minutes on each side or until meat reaches desired doneness (for medium-rare, a thermometer should read 135°; medium, 140°; medium-well, 145°). Allow to stand for 5 minutes before slicing.

Caramel Apple Cider

PREP: 5 MIN. • **COOK:** 2 HOURS
MAKES: 12 SERVINGS (¾ CUP EACH)

INGREDIENTS

- 8 cups apple cider or juice
- 1 cup caramel flavoring syrup
- ¼ cup lemon juice
- 1 vanilla bean
- 2 cinnamon sticks (3 inches)
- 1 tablespoon whole allspice
  Whipped cream, hot caramel ice cream topping and cinnamon sticks, optional

DIRECTIONS

1. In a 3-qt. slow cooker, combine the apple cider, caramel syrup and lemon juice. Split vanilla bean and scrape seeds; add seeds to cider mixture. Place the bean, cinnamon sticks and allspice on a double thickness of cheesecloth; bring up corners of cloth and tie with string to form a bag. Add to cider mixture.

2. Cover and cook on low for 2-3 hours or until heated through. Discard spice bag. Pour cider into mugs; garnish with whipped cream, caramel topping and additional cinnamon sticks if desired.

BUTTERSCOTCH MULLED CIDER Combine the cider with 1 cup of butterscotch schnapps liqueur and 4 cinnamon sticks. Heat as directed.

HARVEST CIDER Substitute 4 cups pineapple juice for half of the cider. Stud an orange wheel with 8 whole cloves; add to juices with 1 cinnamon stick and 1 tea bag. Heat as directed.

Oh-So-Good Creamy Mashed Potatoes

PREP: 20 MIN. • **COOK:** 25 MIN. • **MAKES:** 18 SERVINGS (¾ CUP EACH)

INGREDIENTS

- 8 large Yukon Gold potatoes, peeled and quartered (about 6 pounds)
- 2 teaspoons salt
- 2½ cups 2% milk
- ½ cup butter, cubed
- 3 teaspoons garlic salt
- 1 teaspoon pepper
- ¼ cup sour cream
- Additional 2% milk, optional
- Chopped fresh parsley

DIRECTIONS

1. Place potatoes and salt in a stockpot; add water to cover. Bring to a boil. Reduce the heat; cook, uncovered, for 20-25 minutes or until potatoes are tender. Meanwhile, in a large saucepan, heat milk, butter, garlic salt and pepper over medium heat until butter is melted.

2. Drain the potatoes, then shake over low heat for 1-2 minutes to dry. Mash potatoes with a potato masher or beat with a mixer; gradually add the milk mixture. Stir in sour cream. Stir in additional milk to thin if desired. Sprinkle with parsley.

Handcrafted with Love

CREATE A FEELING OF HOME

Hand-Rolled Beeswax Candles

These beautiful, long-burning candles make a thoughtful holiday or hostess gift. Easy to make, they're said to instill a sense of calm when lit, so keep a few for your table, too.

WHAT YOU'LL NEED
16x8-in. beeswax craft sheet*
⅔ wick (about 18 in. per pair)

DIRECTIONS
1. Leave wax sheet out at room temperature for several hours.

2. Cut wick to approximately 9 in.

3. Cut wax sheet in half crosswise.

4. For each candle: Place wick along wax edge, leaving about 1 in. hanging off the candle top. Roll wax tightly and evenly around wick, keeping top and bottom edges of candle even. Roll completely; press gently along the seam with fingertips to secure.

Available online. Ours are from brushymountainbeefarm.com.

Peppermint Lip Balm

You can purchase lip balm tubes online for this fun DIY gift project.

WHAT YOU'LL NEED

- **1 tablespoon shea butter**
- **1 tablespoon beeswax pellets**
- **1 tablespoon sweet almond oil**
- **4 drops food-grade peppermint essential oil**
- **2 droppers**
- **5 lip balm tubes**
- **Microwave-safe dish**
- **Festive patterned paper for labels**
- **Glue stick**

DIRECTIONS

1. Combine the shea butter, wax and oils in dish and heat in microwave for 30 seconds or until completely melted.

2. Use clean dropper to fill the lip balm tubes. Stand upright; let cool completely.

3. Wrap containers with labels and secure with glue.

Winter Wonderland Teacups

Create magical winter fairy gardens with vintage teacups and found objects. They're simple enough that you could send one home with every guest as a sweet holiday memento.

DIRECTIONS

Fill clean china cups with glass decorator marbles. Cover with thin white cotton batting or precut paper snowflakes. Decorate each teacup scene with miniature creatures, houses, trees, vintage ornaments and artificial snow, as desired.

Random Acts of Christmas

Find an old soda crate, round up some canning jars, then count down to the 25th with one good deed a day.
Wide-mouth half-pint mason jars should fit nicely into most vintage soda crates, but test them before getting started.

WHAT YOU'LL NEED

- **Wooden soda crate**
- **2 keyhole hangers with screws and anchors**
- **24 half-pint mason jars**
- **Decorative papers**
- **Chipboard or sticker numbers**
- **24 acts of kindness ideas, written out on individual strips of paper**
- **Trinkets, toys or candy to coordinate with paper strips**
- **Christmas garland, optional**
- **Metal barn star for topper**
- **Power drill**
- **Craft glue**
- **Hot glue gun**
- **Silver metallic spray paint, optional**

DIRECTIONS

1. Use power drill to install 2 keyhole hangers on back side of crate. Measure and mark for each hole first. For best results, be sure both screws go through the back side of crate and into one of the vertical dividers for the compartments.

2. Use mason jar lid as a guide to trace and cut out circles from decorative papers. With decorative side facing outward, center a paper circle on the inside of each lid. Adhere with craft glue.

3. Fill each jar with a trinket, toy, candy or suggested act of kindness.

4. Screw lids on jars. Center numbers on lids. Adhere with craft glue. Add garland embellishment if desired. Place jars in numbered order inside crate compartments.

5. Add star topper and secure in place with hot glue. (If desired, paint star with silver metallic spray paint before attaching to crate.)

Shovel snow for a neighbor.

Wrap presents for grandparents.

Spread some fa-la-la: go caroling!

Lift someone's spirit with a merry homemade card.

Trim a tree!

Give candy canes of kindness to mail carriers, garbage collectors, babysitters, etc.

Make jolly cookies for friends.

"Strong is the tree that bends with the wind, then bounces back again."

Jo Ann Fazenbaker
Oakland, Maryland